Henry Foley

Jesuits in Conflict

Historic Facts

Henry Foley

Jesuits in Conflict
Historic Facts

ISBN/EAN: 9783744704717

Printed in Europe, USA, Canada, Australia, Japan

Cover: Foto ©Lupo / pixelio.de

More available books at **www.hansebooks.com**

See page 64.

OR
HISTORIC FACTS

Illustrative of the labours and sufferings of the English Mission and Province of the Society of Jesus.

IN THE TIMES OF
QUEEN ELIZABETH AND HER SUCCESSORS.

First Series.

I. THOMAS POUNDE, OF BELMONT, S.J., *Confessor of the Faith.*
II. GEORGE GILBERT, OF SUFFOLK, S.J., *Confessor of the Faith and Ex*
III. FATHER THOMAS DARBYSHIRE, S.J., *Exile for the Faith.*

BY A MEMBER OF THE SOCIETY OF JESUS.

"*Lapidati sunt, secti sunt, tentati sunt, in occisione gladii mortui sunt, circuierunt in melotis, in pellibus caprinis, egentes, angustiati, afflicti.*"—Epist. ad Heb. xi. 37.

LONDON: BURNS AND OATES.

1873.

PREFACE.

It may be said, without fear of exaggeration, that the history of England, since the [so-called] Reformation, has yet to be written. So long as the Catholics of this country were subjected to the savage and exterminating action of the penal laws, not only were they robbed of their privileges as Englishmen, but their very existence was rendered precarious, and a Catholic literature impossible. On the other hand, every record of the heroic lives or virtuous deeds of Catholics was studiously suppressed, or maliciously misrepresented, in order to justify, by a gigantic falsehood, the most atrocious cruelties and injustice, and so conceal from the English nation at large the fact that they were sanctioning a persecution of Christians as barbarous and inhuman as any that was ever inflicted in Pagan times on the Spouse of Christ.

But the circumstances of the Catholics of England have changed, and, under the milder forms of social, which have succeeded to those of political, persecution, they are able to collect and publish their chronicles, to review their past, and study their future. Simultaneously with this increase of opportunities for telling the truth, has arisen a corresponding increase in the disposition of their fellow-citizens to listen to it; and the access recently granted to public and private collections of authentic documents has opened the sources of history to general inquiry. One by one the lives and deeds of men who have laboured and suffered for the Faith, or borne witness to it by their blood, are emerging from their obscurity and asserting their rightful place in English history, exciting, at the same time, both the gratitude and devotion of Catholics towards those who have fought so good a fight in the cause of truth, and the execration of every honest and impartial reader at the cruelties perpetrated on them in the name of English law.

The present volume is intended to form the first of a series of publications illustrative of the history of the Society of Jesus in the

English mission and province, and embracing the lives of various distinguished Jesuit Martyrs and Confessors of the Faith, with many interesting historical facts connected with the Society of Jesus in particular, and the Catholic community in England in general. These will commence from the time of Fathers Robert Parsons and Edmund Campion (the blessed Martyr), who were first sent with others into England by His Holiness Pope Gregory XIII., A.D. 1580, to encourage and confirm the afflicted Catholics of England then groaning under the terrible weight of an unprecedented persecution, and to promote and keep alive in this country the Catholic religion of our forefathers which was struggling for existence under the exterminating enactments of Queen Elizabeth.

Manresa House, Roehampton,
Feast of St. Bartholomew Apostle, 1873.

INDEX.

	PAGE
INTRODUCTORY CHAPTER	1
THOMAS POUNDE, OF BELMONT, S.J.	19
GEORGE GILBERT, S.J.	147
FATHER THOMAS DARBYSHIRE, S.J.	215

Facts illustrative of the times of Elizabeth, Queen of England.

INTRODUCTORY CHAPTER.

STRANGE times were the three hundred years of open persecution against Catholics in England. A study of the history of that period, and a reference to the State Papers in the Public Record Offices, both at home and on the Continent, really lead the reader to the conclusion that all the powers of hell, united to the brute force of faithless man, combined to destroy and crush, root and branch out of the land, the ancient faith of our noble ancestors, by means of a series of savage enactments called "*the penal laws*," an analysis of which would appear simply fabulous to the more liberally minded of the present day.

No stronger proof of the divine origin of the persecuted religion of our forefathers is needed than its surviving that dreadful shock of centuries, and the marvellous or rather the supernatural constancy of its afflicted members. A thick black cloud had ascended up from the lower regions, not only deadening and darkening the hearts and understandings of men from the throne to the cottage, but inspiring them with feelings of the most savage cruelty, exceeding in brutality, if possible, the persecuting rage of the Pagan Emperors in the first three hundred years of the existence of the Church!

The hatred of the ancient faith poisoned the very fountains of justice itself; the judges of the land (thank God now of a very different stamp), as though their very lives, offices, and dignities were at stake when Catholics were arraigned, ceased to administer justice, and the poor frightened and degraded "twelve men" were always found willing tools at their beck. The laws of evidence, as may be seen by most of the trials of those times, were wholly set aside. The bare suspicion that a man was a Priest, or a member of the Society of Jesus, was sufficient for his capital conviction. What should we think of the present Prime Minister sending to our distinguished and high-minded Attorney-General the following instructions on the occasion of a great State trial for high treason, involving the lives of multitudes of men of high rank, virtue, and learning. It was in the case of the Gunpowder Plot. There was a strong feeling in the country that the King's (James I.) cruel treatment of, and his base ingratitude towards, his faithful Catholic subjects, to whom both he and his martyred mother owed so much, and whose promises to Catholics he had shamefully broken, was the very cause of the Plot itself, which no doubt it was, driving the Catholics to desperation.*

Domestic, Jac. I., State Papers, Vol. xix., No. 94. P. R. Office.

[Endorsed by Sir Edward Coke. "My Lord of Salisbury's directions touching P. treason"] 160⅝.

"These things I am commanded to refer unto your memory. . . .

"First, that you be sure to make it appear unto ye world yt there was an employment of some p'sons to Spaine for a practise of invasion, as soon as ye Q.'s breath was owt of her body.†

---

* Upon this head see the very valuable and interesting volume by Father Morris, *The Condition of Catholics under James I.*

† This was at least straining at a point. Lingard says, *Hist. of England*, vol. vii., p. 9, that the Catholics almost unanimously supported the right of James I. Amongst the State Papers, *Dom. Jac. I.*, Vol. i., No. 56, 1603, is a most affectionate and loyal address of the Catholics of England to the King on his accession, stating their cruel grievances, and protesting the most loyal obedience. Shortly *before* the death of Elizabeth the representative of an *expiring faction*, which has been called the Spanish party amongst the English Catholics, had arranged with the Ministers of Philip a plan for the invasion of England. *The death of Elizabeth disconcerted the project.* It is true that a few disconcerted individuals remained, two of whom, insignificant persons, were sent to Philip to discover the real dispositions of the Spanish Council soon after James came to England, but they signally failed. At all events, weak as it was, it afforded a point of which the Attorney-General was to make use to aid him in rendering the accused "as fowle in this as you may."

"The reason is this for wch ye K. doth urge it: he saith some men there are yt will give owt, and do, *yt only dispaire of the K.'s courses in* [with] *ye Catholicks, and his severity, drawe all these to souch woorks of discontentment;* where by you it will appear yt before his Maties face was seen, or yt he had don anything in government, the K. of Sp. was moved, though he refused it, saying he rather expected to have peace.

"Next you must in *any case,* when yow speake of the lre [letter] wch was the first growd [ground] of discovery, *absolutely disclaime yt any of these wrote it, thogh yow leave ye further judgment indefinite, who els it shold be.*

"Lastly, and yt yow must not omitt, yow must deliver in commendation of my L. Monteagle, words to show how sincerely he delt, and how fortunately it proved yt he was ye instrument of so great a blessing as this was. To be short, Sr, yow can remember how well ye K. in his book dyd answere his lordship's part in it, from wch sense yow are not to varry, but obiter (as you know best how), to give some eccleo [*eclat*] of yt particular action, in that day of publick triall of these men, because it is so lewdly given out, yt he was once of this Plott of Powder, and afterwards betraied all to me. This is but ex abundanti yt I do troble yow, but as they come to my hedd or knoledge, or yt I am directed, I am not scrupulous to send yow.

"Yow must remember to lay Owen as fowle in this as you may."* 117.

What can be thought of trials based on such infamous instructions from an ungrateful and thankless tyrant, who had declared to one of his attendants "that since Protestants had so generally received and proclaimed him King, he had now no need of Papists"—through an obsequious First Lord of the Treasury—to a notoriously hard-hearted and cruel Attorney-General? What chance, may be asked, had the unfortunate arraigned under such circumstances? It is clear that, right or wrong, a conviction *must* be got, at any cost.

Well would it be if historians adverse to the Catholic faith were to look into these State Papers before writing their uncharitable volumes. Let the charges against Catholics, whether collectively as a body or individually, and the persons making them be fairly examined. And in a majority of cases it will be found that the very absurdity of the former, and the characters of the latter, will afford sufficient refutation. In many cases the accusers are miserable hungry

* The subject of this *dignified* recommendation of the First Lord of the Treasury was, I presume, Nicholas Owen, *alias* Little John, a Jesuit Lay-brother, who died upon the rack in the Tower, where he was divers times hung up for seven hours together, but not a word could they force from his sealed and faithful lips; at length "they tormented him so long and so often, that his bowels gushed out together with his life." This dear and noble martyr was seized at Henlip Castle, with Father Garnet and Father Oldcorne (See Morris' *Condition of Catholics*).

spies, paupers, offering their "valuable services" to, or else in the first instance retained by the Ministers of the day.

To follow out this subject, and publish some of the trials of Catholics in those times, would fill many a volume, and a deeply interesting series it would be, but this is not the scope of the present volume. An inquirer has only to refer to "*The History of the penal laws against Roman Catholics*, &c., by Mr. Madden, 1847," to satisfy himself of the correctness of these assertions. As a further proof, in the time of Elizabeth, to which this volume relates, we need only refer the reader to the following lives, in addition to which two other cases shall be shortly alluded to, viz., (1) that of the blessed martyr Father Arrowsmith, about half a century later, 1628; and (2), close upon our own times, the seven Jesuit martyrs and others, victims of the perjured Oates, &c. In which fearful assault against Catholics in general, but more especially against the members of the Society of Jesus in England, 1678–9, five of these innocent and learned Fathers were dragged from Newgate on hurdles through Holborn, Oxford Street, &c., to Tyburn, and there butchered at one and the same time, on the 30th June, $167\frac{8}{9}$.

1. In the case of Father Arrowsmith, what will be thought of the conduct of Mr. Justice Yelverton, who on the prisoner being summoned before him at the Lancaster Summer Assizes, August, 1628, thus addressed him in the presence of the jury—

"Sirrah, art thou a Priest?" An admission of the fact would of course have capitally convicted him on the spot. On the martyr humbly saying, "I would to God I were worthy," the learned judge repeated his former question. "I would I were," was the answer." "Are you then no Priest?" the prisoner was silent. His lordship addressing the jury, said, "You may plainly see he is a Priest: I warrant you, he would not, for all England, deny his Orders." After this interesting prelude, a certain parson Lee, called by one of the chroniclers of the event, "the limping old minister," who was sitting by the judge on the bench, whispered in his lordship's ear, and then began aloud to revile the accused, as a seducer of the people, and that if some order were not taken with him, he would make half Lancashire Papists. By way of answer, Father Arrowsmith asked leave to be allowed to defend his religion in a disputation with the minister. The judge coarsely refused. On the Father, in reply, offering not only to defend it by words, but that he was ready to seal it with his blood, the honourable judge answered in a savage and insulting manner, that "he should die, and see his own bowels burnt before his face."* The Father replied, "And you, my lord, must die too." After a long scene of this nature, the prisoner was sent back by his

---

* The reader is perhaps aware that one part of the sentence of death was that the poor sufferers should be cut down *alive*, and disembowelled in that state.

lordship to the castle, with an order that he should be put in some dark place, without light or company; and on the keeper saying that he had no such place, he was ordered to put him in the worst he had. It seems that the indictments were not prepared at the above time, for the judge himself, on the removal of Father Arrowsmith from the bar, framed two indictments; one for being a Catholic, the other for being a member of the Society of Jesus. The first was supported only by an infamous woman and her wicked son; the second only by a boy of twelve years of age, son of the above-mentioned minister. The Father was of course found guilty, and received his dreadful sentence; upon which, falling upon his knees, and bowing his head very low, he exclaimed, *Deo gratias*—"God be thanked." He was remanded back to the castle, with the "widow's mite," as they then called it, that is, "a great paire of bolts on his legges."

Mr. Justice Whitlock, the other judge, was so disgusted that he declined to sign the death warrant. To pass over the charge to the jury, and the further infamous and cruel conduct of his lordship towards his victim, pursuing him even after death, it shall only be added that this judge hastened the execution by a day, in order that it might take place before he left Lancaster, that he "stood in a chamber window within the towne, with a pair of spectacles of a longe sight upon his nose, to behoulde the execution, which, when he had seene performed, he called for his dinner, which was aboute two o'clock after middaye, vpon the feaste of St. Augustin—that after dinner there were presented to him two fatt staggs, which, as he did behoulde, admyringe theire fattnesse, the martyr's head and quarters were brought into his sight, where he made uncivill and barbarous comparisons, betwixte the quarters of the one and the other; and that the next daie the judge departed out of the towne, and passinge by the place where the martyr's head was sett amongst other heades, he caused itt to be putt vpon a poule 8 foote, and higher than the rest." This learned judge met with a dreadful death, evidently (as was the general opinion) from the hand of God, on the 24th of January, 1629. He was sitting at supper January 23, 1629–30, when he felt a blow as if some one had struck him on the head; upon which he fell into a rage against the servant behind him, who protested that neither he nor any one else had struck him. A little after, he felt another, like the first, and then in great terror was carried to bed, crying out, "That dog Arrowsmith has killed me." He died the next morning.* So much for this specimen.

2. The second instance we shall quote is that of Oates' victims. It was in vain that the clearest alibi was proved in the case of Father Ireland by an overwhelming array of witnesses of the highest

---

* See Dodd's *Church History*, vol. iii., p. 80. Edit. 1742; Tanner's *Vita et Mors Jesuit. pro fide interfect*; Bishop Challoner's *Missionary Priests*, vol. ii., p. 123.

rank and respectability; and in the case of all the accused, every statement of importance sworn to by the wretched perjurer and his assistants, Bedloe, Dugdale, &c., were discredited; but the Lord Chief Justice Scroggs, and his confrères, either rejected or overruled all, and directed the jury to find the accused guilty. They were perfectly bloodthirsty. These infamous judicial proceedings gave rise to the following skit in *Peveril of the Peak*, very aptly quoted by the late Dr. Oliver in his short notice of Father Whitbread, one of the said victims, and who was at the time the Provincial or Superior of the English members of the Society of Jesus.*

"Who has been hunted on the stern and unmitigable accusations, but has been at last brought to bay? Did high and noble birth, honoured age, and approved benevolence, save the unfortunate *Lord Stafford?* . . . Did subtlety and genius, and the exertions of a numerous sect, save *Fenwick* or *Whitbread*, or any of the accused Priests? Were *Groves*, *Pickering*, or any of the other wretches who have suffered, safe in their obscurity? There is no condition of life, no range of talent, no form of principle which affords protection against an accusation which levels conditions, confounds characters, renders men's virtues their sins, and rates them as dangerous in proportion as they have influence, though attained in the noblest manner and used for the best purposes. Call such a one an accessory to the

* Oliver, *Collectania S.J.*, p. 112.

plot, let him be mouthed in the evidence of *Oates* or *Dugdale*, and the blindest shall foresee the issue of the trial.

"'Prophet of evil,' said *Julian*, 'my father has a shield invulnerable to protect him. He is *innocent!*'

"'Let him plead his innocence at the bar of Heaven,' said the voice; 'it will serve him little where *Scroggs* presides.'

"'Still, I fear not,' said *Julian*, counterfeiting more confidence than he really possessed; 'my father's cause will be pleaded before *twelve Englishmen!*'

"'Better before twelve wild beasts,' answered the invisible, 'than before Englishmen, influenced by party prejudice, passion, and the epidemic terror of an imaginary danger.'"

When men's minds were cooled down by the torrents of innocent and noble blood poured out on that lamentable occasion, the perjurer Oates himself had his day of reckoning. He was soon after indicted on several counts for wilful and corrupt perjury, and found guilty on all, and sentenced to a terrible punishment besides imprisonment for life. The court in passing sentence "lamented that he could not be punished with death in atonement for the innocent blood his perjuries had caused to be shed." In the time of William and Mary, however, this man was pardoned, and actually pensioned with a handsome salary! Most of his other fellow-perjurers met with miserable ends. These legal murderers of such men as Lord Stafford, Archbishop Plunkett, Mr. Langhorne, &c., were so flagrant and infamous, that the minds and better feelings of the nation were shocked. No more public executions for religion took place, though numbers were left to die of their sufferings in the dungeons of London and other cities: a more cruel execution by far, because more lingering. The persecuting spirit was then turned for a time rather against the property than the person of Catholics; as in our own day, since the partial repeal of the penal laws, it has changed to a more deadly, because a more insidious mode of attack, especially in regard to unfortunate workhouse children and prisoners.

If, as before observed, the infernal power stirred up this persecuting rage against the ancient religion of our forefathers; there was also, by way of antidote, poured down from above by a merciful Providence, upon the afflicted Catholics of either sex and of every grade, both priest and layman, monk and nun, young men and maidens, boys and girls, a marvellous spirit of constancy and courage, to enable them to meet the fearful storm. Martyrs went to execution, or rather butchery, and confessors to the prisons and torture, and suffered the loss of their goods and estates with a spirit of joy and determined constancy, which will not yield a jot to that of those who suffered in the first days of Christianity.

The object of the present volume is to draw forth from the shades of obscurity, in which they have been too long buried, three English members of the Society of Jesus, noble characters of the stamp just mentioned.

I. Thomas Pounde, formerly of Belmont, Esquire, who though probably but little known to many of the present day, yet was one of the most, if not *the* most, glorious of the confessors of the faith in England of his time, pregnant as it was with noble champions of the Church. A notice of this remarkable man cannot fail to be historically useful, illustrating in itself, as it does on the one hand, the brutal ferocity and systematic persecution carried on with unrelenting rage by the professors of the reformed religion, of every social grade, against those who held the ancient Catholic faith of our forefathers, to which reference has been made; and on the other, of the terrible afflictions of every kind, in person and property, and the marvellous patience and long suffering of the oppressed Catholics.

To avoid confusion this history will be divided into two heads.

1. The personal history of the confessor, gathered from various sources, Father Bartoli, S.J., *Istoria S. J. l'Inghilterra;* Father Tanner, S.J., *Apostolorum Imitatrix,* and Father Henry More, S.J., *Historia Provinciæ Anglicanæ S. J.,* &c. &c.

2. An account of his connection with Father Edmund Campion, the blessed martyr, and Father Robert Parsons, to whom, and to the Catholic cause generally, he rendered such great assistance. Also,

a copy of his famous "Six reasons," with some interesting letters and papers of his, which have been procured from the State Papers in the Public Record Office, having found their way into that interesting depot from the Sheriff of Wilts, in which county they were seized.

The history of Thomas Pounde, undoubted as are the facts, reads more like a tale of fiction than one of real life. If we consider his wonderful conversion, his long and painful imprisonment of thirty years, shifted from dungeon to dungeon, becoming an inmate of no less than ten or eleven different prisons, the extreme severity exercised towards him, with the self-imposed addition of the severest corporal austerities, his undaunted courage in facing the adversary, his petitioning for and reception into the Society of Jesus in prison, in 1579, spending his whole Religious life there, until 1602–3, when, upon the accession of James I., being released, he was, by order of his Superiors, sent to his paternal mansion at Belmont, and died there in the very same room in which, seventy-six years before, he had first seen the light of day, the whole seems rather the production of man's invention than what it is—the sober record of undoubted facts. As to our confessor's degree in the Society of Jesus, having received a liberal education, partly at Winchester College, and partly in London, studying civil law there to prepare himself for the Bar, and being besides naturally a man of considerable talent, good wit, and ready speech, we may presume that, under ordinary circumstances, his Superiors would have designed him for the degree of the Priesthood, but as his long and unbroken imprisonment rendered this quite impossible, either the Temporal Coadjutors must claim the honour of possessing this great athlete of Christ, or he must be regarded as a Scholastic awaiting an opportunity of being advanced to the Priesthood. We may imagine his making his vows of Religion to Father Weston, *alias* Edmonds, when confined in Wisbeach Castle with him. He may, too, have found occasional opportunities of making the accustomed renovation of vows to our Fathers of the Society or other Priests he may have met with in some of the various prisons, and he may also have made his solemn vows in like manner, though there is no record of the fact. Nevertheless, he truly made a good noviceship!

II. George Gilbert, formerly of Suffolk, Esquire, the dear friend of Thomas Pounde, another noble sample of the same type; an English young gentleman who, having embraced the Catholic faith, in which he had not been brought up, devoted himself to works of charity, and who, more fortunate than his friend Thomas Pounde, after doing all he could for his religion at home, and suffering the confiscation of his ample estates and fortune, being hotly pursued by the pursuivants, retired abroad, and proceeding to Rome, gave himself up to the service of God and his neighbours, intending to enter the Society of Jesus, which he dearly loved and admired. It pleased God to accept this intention; for, being seized with mortal sickness, he was both admitted to the Society as a Novice, and allowed to make the vows of Religion in *articulo mortis.**

III. The Rev. Father Thomas Darbyshire, a learned and eminent Father of the Society of Jesus, and an exile for his faith, and who, under God, was the first means of the conversion of George Gilbert to the true faith. An Oxford man, and in the reign of Mary a high dignitary of the Catholic Church in England. He was nephew of Bonner, the famous Catholic Bishop and confessor, who died of his sufferings in prison under Elizabeth.

* Father Henry More, S.J., *Hist. Prov. Angl. S.J.;* Father Bartoli, *Istoria della Comp. di Gesù Inghilterra;* Father Tanner, *Soc. Jesu Apost. Imitatrix; Life of Campion,* by Robert Simpson, Esq., &c.

Book the First

THOMAS POUNDE, OF BELMONT, S.J.

THOMAS POUNDE, OF BELMONT, S.J.

PART I.

AMONG the companions who followed Father Parsons into the Society was Giles Gallop, who died soon after his admission, being allowed to take his simple vows in *articulo mortis*. Bombinus has made a mistake in name, in counting Brother Giles Gallop among those who were distinguished either by death for the faith, or by great labours undertaken for Christ in England. This honour, on the contrary, is due to Thomas Pounde, who is sometimes found concealing himself under the assumed name of Gallop, Wallop, Duke, and Harrington.*

Whilst Father Campion at Prague, and Father Parsons at Rome, are engaged, the one in the study of piety and divine wisdom, the other in the office of teaching, it will be opportune to revisit England for a little, and to behold, in the person of an invincible

---

* More, *Hist. Prov. Angl.*, l. ii., n. xiv., p. 44. In the terrible times of the open persecution of Catholics, Priests were compelled constantly to change, not only their places of abode and dress, but their names also. Father Henry Garnet, the blessed martyr, had at least six or eight *aliases*.

athlete of Christ, as well the obstinate fury of the heretics against the Catholics as their unshaken constancy in the faith; for nothing can be more striking than, on the one hand, the pertinacity of the former in harassing, and, on the other, the patient perseverance of the latter in enduring their vexations; and finally, a certain loftiness of mind in others, who, nothing alarmed by this species of virulence, offered themselves with magnanimous hearts to similar sufferings; how much more so if we show in the pertinacious hunting down of one man for thirty years that neither was heretical fury abated, nor Catholic constancy weakened. Thomas Pounde presents this spectacle to our eyes, in whom we encounter a man neither of chance nor of other times.*

God, by a most special privilege, would prepare for the Society in England the very hospice wherein she should be born; and this was no other than the public prisons, and, singularly enough, those of the Tower of London and Castle of Wisbeach, the most renowned of all of them. And, to take possession in our name, there were confined in these prisons, for the Catholic faith, men of holy life, who, though none of them had as yet ever seen our habit, but learnt solely by report of our Institute, our life, and our works, demanded, and, as worthy, obtained admission to the Order in the same prisons. Thus we find the Society in England (a good prognostic, faithfully tested, of what was to follow) born in prison,

* More, *Hist. Prov. Angl.*, l. ii., n. xvi., pp. 44, 45.

growing amidst chains, exercised in various torments, and in a brief space made meet to appear in public upon the carts of justice beneath the gallows, where, hung by the neck, her sons preached with the voice and attested by their blood, before innumerable multitudes of auditors and spectators, the verity of the Catholic faith. And, to speak truly, there is no College of ours, however numerous, or however esteemed, whether in learning or in religious observance, or famous in any other regard, that has not just reason to feel a little envy that our seven English, with Campion himself, were all formed in the cells of the Tower of London, all in the best dispositions for that happy lot, to which the greater part of them arrived, viz., to die for the Catholic faith.*

Thomas Pounde was born at Belmont, twelve miles from Winchester, on the 29th of May, 1539. His parents were William Pounde, Esq., and Anna Wriotesley, sister of Thomas, Earl of Southampton. His parents attest of him that he was just born when he lifted his right hand to his head, which was regarded as a future omen of the victorious combatant.

His early years, until his twenty-third, were spent in the usual study of Humanities at the College of

---

* Bartoli, *Inghilterra*, t. i., l. i., cap. xiv., p. 106. Edit. 1825. The seven English members were, Father Thomas Cottam, martyr; Father Thomas Mettam, died at Wisbeach; Thomas Pond; Father Edmund Campion, martyr; Alexander Briant, martyr; James Bosgrave, and John Hart. The two latter were condemned to death with Father Campion, but were reprieved and banished.

our Lady of Winchester. From thence, going to London, he prepared himself for forensic glory and dignity by the study of the law. It is hard to say in which the gratuitous gifts of nature most abounded in him—whether mental or corporal. He appeared, indeed, more comely in each advancing stage of his life and strength, which was set off by the height of his stature and the excellent formation of his limbs, well set, nimble, and strong. He delighted in all gymnastic and corporal exercises, and displayed great agility. In more advanced life, when quite grey haired, he was a man of majestic and venerable aspect; all these graces made him no little favourite with men of high rank. He was richly furnished, too, with all the other gifts of mind becoming an accomplished cavalier—brave, of great courage, most courteous, of exceedingly polite manners, a munificent spender of money, a good orator, and of ready wit. Upon the occasion of a solemn reception of Queen Elizabeth at Winchester College, he addressed Her Majesty in a complimentary poem of his own composition, with great applause. In the art of Latin verse he attained a considerable degree of excellence.

Shortly after becoming master of his own life and expenditure, on the death of his father, eager to succeed at Court, he went into unpardonable excesses in lavishing his paternal estates on those vain delights and hopes, seeing that it pleased the Queen, and being unwilling to be outdone by others. No one will be surprised at this in Elizabeth's reign, seeing the luxury in which she herself indulged, drawing all in her train, and affording in her Court great scope for all those graces and delights of the arts, which belonged to Pounde in so eminent a degree.

He was so careless about his soul that, although a Catholic at heart, yet, in order to gain a footing at Court, he professed outwardly the Queen's religion. The sudden means employed by God, the good Father of all, to bring back to the right path so wretched a wanderer, was an admirable proof of His compassion, using, in order to win him to eternal salvation and to those great merits to which he arrived, the same means by which this silly youth so strenuously strove to bring himself to perdition.

Christmas Day, as was always customary at the Court until Epiphany, in the year 1569* was most remarkable for its festivities; the most magnificent plays, comedies, concerts, dances, and other games were given at the Court under the direction of Pounde himself. There were assembled here the flower of the nobility and of the youth of London, and no small space within the palace was occupied both by the spectators and performers; and the one thought and desire was to spend money there according to each

---

* Bartoli states it 1569, and cites a letter of Pounde in support of the assertion, dated June 3, 1609. Father More makes it 1564. This is, perhaps, a misprint, because farther on Father More himself makes Pounde to be thirty years of age on his retiring from the Court to Belmont, 1569.

one's power, and he who excelled in this was honoured by the Queen. Pounde was the lucky one of the number in the year 1569, being doubly acceptable to the Queen, both on account of his costly expenditure and gracefulness in dancing; so that what with his being so handsome a youth, and his skill in the art of dancing, surpassing all his equals in agility and grace, there was no one who would willingly be seen with him in the dance. He chose one of his most wonderful performances, which was to be the concluding one, and consisted in raising himself in the air as high as possible and standing upright on tiptoe, to spin himself round like a top, in as many turns and as swiftly as his agility and strength would allow, and especially without growing giddy and falling. He performed this exploit in such a manner, and so nimbly, that the whole theatre resounded with shouts of applause. By way of reward the Queen herself with her uncovered hand seized that of Pounde, and then snatching from the Earl of Leicester his costly cap, put it upon his head for fear lest he might catch cold, being heated and in a perspiration from his violent exertions. The triumphal laurels seemed now to crown him, when the Queen, after he had rested himself, invited him to repeat a second time the same dance. Spinning round on tiptoe more quickly than ever, he was seized with giddiness, and fell flat to the ground. The previous applause was changed into shouts of laughter and derision; but what wounded him most was that the Queen, instead of offering her hand to raise him up, as though in anger for thus spoiling the festivity, gave him a kick by the two sarcastic words, "Rise Sir Ox,"* and then turning round, joined the rest in their laughter, to his great confusion. Stung by her words he rose indeed, but lifting himself up on one knee, with his face to the ground, he exclaimed to himself, *sotto voce* [but loud enough to be overheard by others], that solemn sentence, *Sic transit gloria mundi* —"So passeth the glory of this world," and hurrying away, after a very short space leaving London, he deserted the Court and its fallacious hopes, having reaped the reward of its vanities—a wasted property and offended religion. Retiring to his paternal mansion at Belmont, he there buried himself in solitude. Pondering upon the rewards of obsequious slavery to the world, he blamed himself as the most foolish of men, and felt how much more blessedly he would have acted had he consecrated to God, to the

---

* "Rise Sir Ox." Father More, *Hist. Prov. Angl.*, uses the word "Bull." Father Tanner and Father Bartoli use "Ox." The expression has, no doubt, reference to the ceremony of creating a Knight for service to the State, in which case the Sovereign lays the sword of State on the back of the kneeling subject, saying, "Rise, Sir so and so." The Queen's object was to ridicule and humiliate Mr. Pounde, and, in order to do so, she parodies the form of conferring the knighthood. The term is also preferable, because the ox being a clumsy awkward animal, which the bull is not, is often used and applied to express awkwardness in a human subject, and the royal vixen, who was no fool, evidently meant to convey this idea in thus cruelly mortifying her quondam favourite.

affairs of eternity, and to the salvation of his own soul, the things which, in contempt to God, to the disgrace of religion, and to the loss of his own soul, he had so profusely lavished before the eyes of the Queen; finally, from hence he conceived a great self-confusion and horror, and made a resolution of amendment so constant and fixed, that for the ensuing forty-four years (he was than aged thirty) he lived altogether as another man. Before all things, therefore, he procured to be reconciled to God and the Church, making restitution by the most fervent penance for his shameful denial of both before the eyes of the Court, by simulating the heresy of the Queen. He exchanged his paternal mansion for the private house of a Catholic citizen, in which for a little more than two years he practised the solitude of a hermit, giving himself to prayer and austerity of life, and self-examination, despising what others either thought or said of him, or of his adopted manner of life, suffering much from his friends, and from himself too, whilst he thus as it were acclimated himself both to solitude, charity, neglect of the necessaries of life, and to other severity and hard treatment. He also bound himself by vow to perpetual chastity, and to embrace the Priesthood, after proving himself worthy of it by a seven years' trial in the exercise of pious works.

It was then also that he sought entrance into the Society of Jesus, being attacted to it chiefly on account of its abstaining from accepting dignities, its vows of obedience, its devotion to the Holy See, &c. He had also read letters from our Fathers in the Indies, with an account of their labours and sufferings there, and the numerous conversions of those barbarous idolators to the faith, whom God in His mercy had drawn to Himself. The reading of these letters greatly increased his desire of entering the Society, and devoting himself wholly to it, as a son and servant.

This is the time to which we must refer those things which are related of him by our Father Thomas Stephens (of whom more hereafter) in his petition to Father General Mercurianus in 1578, for Pounde's admission into the Society, which is related further on. As we shall find recorded more fully in the petition of Father Stephens, he lived for two years, and a little more, in the severe mode of life there mentioned, more like a hermit, occupied with himself and the care of his soul. Sometimes, for several hours in the day, imparting his fervent spirit to his neighbour abroad, reserving the night for his prayers, and remitting nothing of his accustomed austerities. In helping Protestants he would make it a point to endeavour to withdraw them from their personal antipathy to himself, and their accustomed injustice towards Catholics, joining at the same time, with the grace of God, his own particular talent of speaking and power of persuasion; he thus raised many that were fallen and vacillating, and re-established them in the ancient faith.

Whilst Pounde was thus burning with zeal for serving souls, Father Henry Alvarez returning into England from Rome, related to him many things regarding the Institute of the Society, its ardent zeal in helping its neighbour, its strict rule of obedience, its devotion to the Holy See, its refusal of all dignities, &c., by all of which the mind of Thomas was so inflamed with the desire of embracing its mode of life, that had not his aged mother, who yet survived, been an obstacle, he would have given away his property to the poor (which otherwise would have been confiscated to the Treasury on his departure) and instantly have embarked for Rome, where was the Novitiate of the Society.

In the meantime God sent him, in the first instance, as an acquaintance, which grew afterwards into the closest friendship, a youth named Thomas Stephens, a native of the diocese of Salisbury. I do not know whether he also, like Pounde, was inflamed by a desire to enter the Society by reading our accounts from India, but we find him a little later sailing to the East, and there for forty years engaged in Apostolic and most meritorious labours in the neighbourhood of Goa, for the salvation of those blind idolators whom he enlightened by preaching the Gospel, so as to form one of the most numerous and pious Christian congregations that flourished in those parts of India. He was by birth of a respectable family well known to Pounde, who gave him an asylum in his house, treating him as his equal; but for the benefit of both they mutually agreed to appear abroad, Pounde in quality of master, Stephens in the habit and employ of a servant. This they did as a blind to the Protestants, who watched with a thousand eyes the footsteps of those Catholics who were well dressed, and seemed to be in good circumstances, in order to oppress them, and enrich themselves with their substance.

Thus they lived together for nearly two years, when, impatient of further delay in accomplishing the desire of their hearts towards the Society, they resolved to leave their affairs to chance, and to break through all the hindrances that too much retarded them. Then collecting together what ready money they could raise by the sale of such things as they had at hand, they held themselves in readiness to seize the first good opportunity of secretly leaving England, and with a select band of youths whom Pounde had gained to God and the Society. Nay, further, he had determined, should he get over to the neighbouring port, Calais, to more than double that number, and to that end, to spend two or three months in France and Flanders, in searching out the flower of the English youth that were there, and collecting what Providence should give him, to conduct them to Rome at his own expense, and there to offer himself and them to the General of the Society as his sons and subjects.

Departing for London in order to arrange affairs and remove all hindrances to their embarking, out of compassion to his host, who was also a friend of his, he delayed some time there in order to convert him from heresy, and spent some nights in argument with him; but by this man's obstinacy everything was overturned. Pounde at length determined at daybreak the next morning to embark on the Thames for his proposed voyage. But man proposes, God disposes; and so in this instance it was not to be as our confessor had determined, but it pleased God to make an entirely opposite disposal, and to ordain that this very friend and host should be the means of reserving him for a dreadful imprisonment of thirty years!

On that very same evening Pounde was summoned by an officer of the pseudo-Bishop of London, Sandys, to render an account of the manner in which he observed the Queen's laws: no crime was charged against him, no accusation made, nor proof given of any violation of the law. Pounde followed his conductor to prison, with a countenance as calm, and a courage as great, as though embarking for Italy.

In reference to this wonderful equanimity in our glorious confessor, Father Bartoli observes upon the fact of his being thus completely cut off, within one night of its accomplishment, from the hope of offering himself as a member of the Society, for which he had waited four years. How fervent that desire was, Pounde himself, on a subsequent occasion, when he had already pined for two years in prison and had been tortured beyond ordinary custom, whereby his body was reduced to a wretched condition, sent to protest to our Very Reverend Father General that all his sufferings were as nothing in comparison with his interior grief to see himself deprived of the grace of being one of his sons, for which he had sighed for six years.

Pounde, nevertheless, foresaw that he would incur death should they seize upon his writings against the heretics and the Queen's authority in matters ecclesiastical, which he carried with him in his bag. The real cause of his imprisonment would seem to have been the exhortations he made to Catholics resolutely to refuse heretical communion, especially in the episcopal city of Winchester, whither he frequently made excursions, and with great zeal confirmed the recusants in their resolutions—to which cause may be added a suspicion of his intention to leave England for Catholic countries, in detecting which the episcopal treasury was greatly interested, as it would lead to the confiscation of Pounde's estate, to the enrichment of the said treasury.

His before-mentioned friend and host was so moved by the incredible constancy of soul of our prisoner, that, although no previous force of argument by Pounde could conquer him, yet now one special address alone, together with the clear exhibition of Catholic generosity presented by his friend, caused him, with his wife and whole family, to be reconciled to the Church. We may imagine how great was the consolation thus afforded to the sufferer!

In addition to the slight suspicions at first entertained against our confessor, new accusations and strong proofs were now produced. In prison he sustained a long assault from the bland and courteous speeches of the pseudo-bishop, who offered to release him if he would, for the satisfaction of the public, really show himself once at church, and be present at a Protestant sermon. He with great prudence returned him word for word as a gentleman, candidly saying, "If I cannot recover my liberty otherwise than by offending God, I am firmly resolved that my soul shall be first torn from my body, than that my body shall go forth from prison on such terms."

The fruit of this noble reply was, that he remained in prison for six months. He was then liberated on bail, through the intervention of his relative the Earl of Southampton, who became his surety that he should not leave the country, nor interfere with affairs of religion, but confining himself to his house at Belmont, should peremptorily appear if, and when cited, within twenty days.* The condition of the

* The following is copied from the State Papers, *Dom. Eliz.*, Vol. cc., No. 59, P. R. O.—"7 December, 1585. Thomas Pownde and Ellen his mother, bounde in a 100 markes that the said Thomas Pounde shall remain at his mother's house in Kennyton in the countie of Surry." Father Henry More gives Thomas Pounde's mother's name as *Anne*. There may be some misnomer in the case, or Ellen may have been a second name. The above notice of bail can hardly be mistaken as applying to the subject of our history, although it does not appear on what occasion that privilege of bail was granted. One can scarcely gather from the general history that Mr. Pounde was ever out of prison after he so severely handled and gravelled my Lord Horne of Winchester. However the case may be, the extract is given.

recognizance was faithfully kept, except in one regard, which of all others the adversary could not brook, viz., to enlighten with the truths of faith those who were blinded by the errors of heresy, and to confirm the wavering Catholics, all of which he never ceased to do. He associated to himself as companions in his labours and merits, George Cotton, Henry Sudall, and some other gentlemen residing near Belmont. Father More also mentions at this period, a case of exorcism of a certain merchant who lived in the hamlet of St. Mark, who was possessed by an evil spirit, and had desired privately to be freed by the prayers of the Church, to whom Pounde hastened, fortified with relics of the Saints, and with whom he piously discoursed upon the power of the Church against evil spirits, and of the necessity of firmly retaining the right faith. This fact having got wind, and being reported to London, hastened on Pounde's final apprehension.

After he had been for sixteen months at liberty engaged in these pious works, Horne, the pseudo-Bishop of Winchester, under whose jurisdiction our confessor was, ordered him to be seized and sent to prison, together with the other Catholic gentlemen, his companions, who, no few in number, were men of known respectability and probity of life. He summoned them to appear before him, first sending with pretended and fraudulent piety to persuade them that by a too free speaking during their examination, they would do great injury to the common cause of the

Roman religion, and in particular to themselves personally. Being deceived by this stratagem, they remained silent during his civilly-composed address of admonitions, instructions, insults, blasphemies, and boastings, and whatever else came to his tongue. Having thus glutted himself with speaking, he remanded them back to prison, bragging to all that he had, by force of his authority, and his sage reasonings, rendered them mute and ashamed of themselves, so that they had not the courage to breathe a word before him. The assembled court insolently and contumaciously called them "dumb Catholic dogs," attributing their silence to the weakness of their cause and their own ignorance. But the prisoners being already informed by the Catholics of the bishop's treachery, were eager to recover what had been done by the same game the next day. Being again brought up, the bishop had scarcely begun to speak, when Pounde, taking the word from his mouth, contradicted by the testimony of Vincent of Lerins, the false and maliciously delivered exposition alleged by Horne, to the prejudice of the Roman Catholic faith, upholding Vincent as the champion of the Catholic cause and the great adversary of the heretics. There were present a multitude of spectators of all degrees, both Catholic and Protestant, as many as the large court could hold, drawn thither by the report of this solemn act, and curious to see so many personages of rank in the condition of criminals, thus exposed to disgrace by a man of lower than ordinary stamp, as the greater part of these pseudo-bishops were at that period.

Now, when Horne found himself in a dilemma between the necessity of replying to what he was ignorant of, or of remaining silent and disgraced before so numerous a court, he ran away from the question; and, as though led off by zeal and the obligation of sustaining the dignity of his position, he broke out into insults, and turned upon Pounde a volume of abuse of the worst kind that an angry man knows how to utter. Our confessor, on the contrary, was as composed in countenance as in soul; and, as though the storm was not meant for him, mildly begged of the bishop an answer in reply to his argument, adding to his own, the request of the rest, who took courage by his example. The Catholics made a stir in the court and applauded, while the heretics, not by whispers only, expressed astonishment at the bishop's malice. Horne became like one demented, and though he spoke, yet he understood not what he said, uttering his words incoherently and indistinctly, as one gurgling; and it rather seemed to be a number of spirits in him, than really himself, sending fourth sounds all at one and the same time out of one and the same mouth. The prisoners appeared before him no more, neither at that or any subsequent time; because the bishop, grown wise at his own cost, after retaining them for a couple of months to suffer in divers prisons, to avoid any further adventure with Pounde, handed him and the rest over to the arm of the secular judges, who, being doubtful as to the Queen's wishes regarding the Catholic laymen in general, remanded them to a prison in London. This prison was the Marshalsea, as appears by a list of prisoners there amongst the State Papers, *Dom. Eliz.*, 1580, Vol. 140, No. 40. "Prisoners in the Marshalsea, Thomas Pound, Gent., sent in by a warrant from the Bisshop of Winchester for Papistry the xith of Marche, ano. 1576."

According to Father More, the following were then the most celebrated prisons in London,* viz., three at the three gates of the City—at the gate called Newgate; at that called Lud, from one Luddi, to whom some refer the origin of the City itself; and at the gate called of the house, Gate-house, Westminster, formerly the Western gate of the Monastery. On the other side the Thames there were five—the Bench, or the seat, of the King, King's-bench; that of the chief Magistrate's, called the Marshalsea, or the seat of the Mareshall; the Hall of Winchester, commonly called the Clink; the White Lion, and the Counter (house of reckoning, Nomisterion or Computorium). There were three others scattered through the City—the Fleet, so called from a running stream or ditch of water; another Nomisterion or Counter (in the Poultry), and St. Bridget's Fountain, in which debtors and vagrants were confined; lastly, at the eastern extremity of the City, a projecting fortress, called the Tower of London, which was used for

* More, *Hist. Prov. Angl.*, l. ii., n. xix., p. 48.

the confinement of delinquents of the higher class, traitors, assassins, and the greater offences. Here Pounde was confined three times, and spent altogether three years in it. He found it more like a sepulchre than a prison; he was immured in underground cells, frozen, damp, and stinking, very small, and without a single breathing-hole to admit a ray of light. To Newgate, for the most part, were committed robbers, murderers, witches, and the common sink of all the rogues of London. Our confessor found no prison so odious as this was.

Of what happened to him in the various prisons in which he accomplished his continued martyrdom of thirty years, he is stated by Father Bartoli to have left behind him some precious recollections in a daily journal of fifty chapters, which has been most probably lost.

We now proceed to notice how God was pleased to strengthen His servant as a preparation for his long martyrdom, redoubling his courage and consoling him by bestowing upon him the greatest favour he could desire upon earth, which was to be admitted into the Society of Jesus, and as far as he could do so in his various prisons, and ultimately at Belmont, his own native place, to live as a Religious, like ours in the Novitiate and Colleges. In 1575, Thomas deputed to Rome his friend Stephens to lay before our Very Reverend Father General his long standing desire, and his humble petition to be admitted amongst his sons. He prayed his Paternity "not to refuse this favour because far away and unknown, seeing that whilst God had called him to the Society, though known to him only by report, he had at the same time given him reasons for choosing it; that the Society would not refuse him, though it was unknown to him otherwise than by the account Stephens had given him; that should it ever happen to him that he should become his, and get his foot out of prison and out of England, his Paternity should see him kneeling at his feet; as to the rest, the last of all, though in the love of a son, he was, in the obedience of a subject, indeed amongst the first; and that, should it please God so to honour him as to permit him to die for the confession of the Catholic faith, a thing so imminent, it would be but just that he should in death, as in life, be totally his." With this good embassage, Stephens arrived in Rome: his loyalty to his dear friend, and his fidelity to him as his servant, leave us no room to doubt but that he duly laid the case before the Father General, though, for whatever cause, without success as regards Pounde's petition. He (Stephens) was more fortunate in conducting his own cause, which was the same as that of his patron, for he pleaded it so efficaciously as to obtain permission to be clothed a novice at S. Andrea's on the 20th of October of the same year, 1575.

Three years later, upon renewed and more cogent entreaties on the part of Pounde, Stephens presented in writing to the same Very Reverend Father General, so admirable and well attested an account of the life, the virtues, and other remarkable qualities of Pounde which rendered him a worthy candidate for admission into the Society, that within a few days his petition was granted, and in so extraordinary a case he was able to be dispensed from the ordinary laws of the Society. The following is a translation of a copy of the original in the Archives de l'Etat (Public Record Office), Brussels, varia S.J. (in the valuable collection of Rev. Father Richard Cardwell, *Collectio Cardwelli*, vol. i., p. 16, et seq., Stonyhurst Collection). This interesting document deserves to be given in full, although some apology must be made for a few occasional short repetitions of facts recorded, which have been introduced by the historians from whom this Life has been partly compiled, and which cannot well be erased without interfering with the thread of the narrative.

"I.H.S. *sit nobis* I.H.S.

"The Petition of Mr. Thomas Pounde to the Very Reverend Father General of the Society of Jesus, with a testimonial of his life and conversation.

"Rev. Father in Christ,—Your Paternity knows by name Mr. Thomas Pounde, an Englishman, distinguished by his relationship to the Earl of Southampton; who, when twelve years ago, being summoned by the Queen to Court, enjoyed great influence and favour with Her Majesty, and was detained there in promoting Court plays, games, and dances, and other such like worldly vanities.

"After a few years the divine mercy efficaciously operated in him, and, led by a singular spirit of penitence, withdrew from the Court and all its concerns, and, in the house of a certain relation of his, far away, where, at first indeed, in concealment for two years, he atoned for his past life in pious reading, in watchings, and prayers. But shortly after, without remitting anything of his penitential practices, but mixing somewhat more familiarly in society, in this manner of life showed such examples and proofs of the orthodox truth that he gained many souls, and sought by every means that mode of life, by following which he could the better and more efficaciously employ himself in the divine service and the good of his neighbour.

"In consequence of having read letters of ours from the Indies, and hearing the good fame of the Society, he resolved, after consulting with Father Henry Alvarez, an English Priest of the Society, and a former pupil of Rev. Father Tolet [afterwards Cardinal] who had then just arrived from Rome, to proceed there and enter the Society. He therefore converted into cash, for pious uses, all the property he was able, his mother being yet alive, intending to follow that course concerning his inheritance which the Superiors of the Society should ordain. And when he was, as it were, just upon the point of accomplishing his design, he was recognized by the heretics, upon a certain occasion, which we shall speak of in its proper place, apprehended and cast into prison, and thus deprived of all hope of liberty and of going to Rome.

"He begs of your Paternity that (since he has for so many years had it in heart and desire to enter the Society, and seeing that he cannot get out of prison) you will be satisfied with such his desire and endeavour, and although absent and unknown, having regard to the longing after and zeal for souls that is in him, you will be pleased to admit him to the Society.

"I also, Thomas Stephens, your Paternity's unworthy son, humbly beg this favour for my said master, conjointly with whom for two years, more or less, in the world, I entertained this same intention, of both of us going to Rome and giving ourselves up to the Society. Being well acquainted with his life and conversation, I remark the following facts—When I first turned my thoughts to the Society, Divine Providence so ordained it that I should become acquainted with the said Mr. Thomas; and although out of doors I assumed the character of his servant (both because this better suited my means, as well, and chiefly, by way of a blind to the inquisitive Protestants), yet indoors I lived as his guest in common; excepting, however, the austerities which his more fervent desire of living to God, led him to exercise upon himself.

"*In primis*—as to what relates to his person and estate. He is the only son and heir of his father, a Catholic, but his mother being still alive, as yet enjoys the paternal mansion and estates which fell to him at his death. He is thirty-eight years of age, of a tall and handsome figure, a flowing beard, and a pleasing countenance. In the prison he dresses most handsomely, thinking thus to inspire Catholics with greater courage, and possibly conciliate authority. He has not yet made his philosophy, but is well up in his humanities, and wonderfully addicted to the study of the holy Fathers. He is eloquent in his native tongue, and equally fluent in speaking and writing, and exceedingly efficacious in the art of exhorting and persuasion. When living together, he requested me in frequent conversations to promote this his affair, to the best of my power, when, and as the ocasion should offer; and he afterwards repeated the same in letters, which I hear he sent to my brother and others. For the greater part of the time I lived with him (I speak only to what I have myself witnessed) he used to impose severe austerities upon himself: the ground was his miserable bed; he spent in prayer, with great spiritual gust, one hour at midnight, followed by spiritual reading at daybreak. He would then resume his meditation for two, three, and four hours, spending the rest of the day in reading the holy Fathers, besides two or three hours in prayer in the evening; so that the heretics reported him mad, or a fool, or superstitious; his domestics, and some of his friends also, reported the same of him, calling it imprudent severity against himself, &c., all of which he constantly disregarded with a courageous heart, persevering in his mode of life, giving them example, and causing them to change their reproaches into admiration.

"As often as the opportunity of a Priest allowed it, he would go to confession and Holy Communion on all Sundays and festivals, and frequently in the week, and he was the cause of others doing the same, very frequently complaining to his friends, that Catholics incurring so small a risk to their temporal interests (as it seemed to him), and standing in such great peril of their souls, should so seldom frequent those divine mysteries.

"The episcopal city of Winchester lay not far distant from his house. Happening to hear that many poor Catholic recusants (so the heretics call all those who refuse fellowship with them) lay concealed there, and that a certain aged Priest also dwelt in that city, but who seldom said Mass, and much more seldom communicated them, he quickly betook himself thither, examined into their state and mode of life, provided dinner for them after Mass and Holy Communion, and gave alms to the Priest, exhorting him to celebrate more frequently for the purpose of communicating the Catholics. A little after the returning markets, and at no small expense, he would buy a large stock of cheese, and distribute two or three of these to each of the poor people, stipulating that if they did not choose to respond with greater fervour to the divine privilege, and the grace bestowed upon them, they might regard this as done out of friendship.

"It afforded him wonderful joy and consolation of soul when at times he beheld twelve or sixteen young men of rank, whom he had collected together, hearing Mass, which he had secretly procured to be said in his private oratory, and going to Holy Communion with him.

"He was so assiduous in almsgiving, that besides the daily occasions of beneficence, which he prosecuted in a wonderful manner, he would esteem it a favour if any one gave him information of any Catholic labouring under distress; having always on his lips those words of St. Paul, *Maxime erga domesticos fidei*—'Especially towards the household of faith.' Hence, reckoning as nothing what he was himself able to do, he would most earnestly beg of any of his more wealthy friends, alms for the suffering or incarcerated Catholics, with whom the prisons in London were crowded. I remember his once composing an entire treatise (addressed as a thank-offering to a certain Catholic), expressing his opinion that almsgiving is often beneficial to heretics themselves, because by softening their hearts, their ears are more open to the truth. This treatise he sent for perusal to his most Catholic relation, the Earl of Southampton, who without comparison was then the most illustrious and leading

Catholic in England, and a great supporter of the Faithful.

"I must not omit an arrangement which he made, and although it could not be carried out, it was a strong proof of his love of, and great desire for, the Society. When he was recently apprehended, and was ignorant of what the judges would decide regarding him, he was so composed in mind as immediately to make his will, in which, besides the rest of his property, which he desired to be distributed amongst the poor imprisoned Catholics, he gave £300 to that House or College of the Society in which I might then be, for thither he himself, should this ever be possible, hoped also to be received.

"He daily strove to reconcile enemies; to convert heretics to the true faith; schismatics to a sincere profession of the faith and Catholic practices, with such success, that within a few months (even after such imprisonment) nearly twenty of both sexes, of various ages and conditions in life, were converted by his labours from schismatical tepidity to Catholic piety, and to the bosom of the holy Roman Catholic Church.

"At this period, being now relieved from prison, in the renewed hope of being able in a short time to make his intended journey, he resolved to spend some days, together with the rest of his companions, in prayer and fasting, in order that he might more auspiciously enter upon so important a work, and with greater fervour. I heard him say that he had intended to spend two or three months in Flanders and France, and if he could there pick up young men of good promise, and of his own stamp, to take them with him to Rome, at his own expense, and offer them, with himself, to the Society. He entertained I know not what hopes of converting a certain heretic in London, deeming it a thing very grateful to God, and fitting to render his undertaking auspicious, if, in the meantime, pending the necessary arrangements for his journey, he might by the way effect this good work. He spent that night, therefore, as secretly as possible (so he thought) in the house of the Protestant, for the sake of exhorting and instructing him; but as his labour and pains seemed to be thrown away, with this idea he prepared to leave the house the following day, when, lo! he was unexpectedly apprehended by the pursuivants, taken before the pseudo-Bishop of London, and by him committed to prison.

"His courage of soul on this occasion was remarkable, for when he was cut off from so great a hope of his journey, and exposed to such manifest danger of life (many writings and pamphlets being found upon him by which the heretics would be able to convict him of high treason), yet was he nothing alarmed, nothing changed, but wished all to be referred *ad majorem Dei gloriam*, and to the honour of the Catholic Church, testifying that he, and all his, depended upon the Divine will and Providence. This tended to confirm him in the esteem and good opinion of many, who, as in the former times, never remembered to have observed in him any sign of trouble or dejection of heart, so now they found that these kinds of imperfections were equally remote from his breast.

"The Protestant in whose house he was seized, observing all these things, and struck with veneration at his constancy and piety, at the same time reflecting that all this had happened to him on his account, returning home was converted, and embraced the Catholic faith, and after a few months though with greater difficulty his wife, and not long after his daughters followed his example.

"It was no obscure mark of a sincere conscience in one seeking only the glory of God, that on the pseudo-bishop offering to liberate him if he would promise in his presence just to go once to the church, or to hear a sermon, he replied that, if he could not gain his liberty but by the offence of God and scandalizing his neighbour, he would prefer that his soul should be torn from his body rather than that his body should be released on such terms.

"After six months, at the intervention of the said Earl of Southampton, he was liberated from prison, with leave to go to any part within the kingdom he wished, bail being given to appear within twenty days whenever called upon, and not to meddle with matters of religion, or to quit the realm. He, however, as though he felt himself as secure as formerly from all dangers, went about with greater fervour than ever, strengthening the weak and confirming the strong. Wherefore, after sixteen months, he was summoned to Winchester by the bishop of that city, together with his highly respectable neighbour, George Cotton, Mr. Henry Udall, Mr. Henry Sheldon, and not a few others of his county, men of high family (this, however, I did not see myself, but received it from others who were present, and were very fervent in their commendation of him). And when before the bishop, and a great assembly of spectators, he rendered so brilliant a reason for his faith in the presence of them all, and so severely rebuked the bishop himself, that he was utterly unable, for very rage and confusion, to say a word in reply. The rest of them, no doubt, animated by his powerful eloquence and address, behaved most firmly; so that many who had flocked thither, amazed at the unusual spectacle of so many respectable men placed in such circumstances, left the court favourably inclined to Catholicism.

"After this they were all given into separate custody, and Mr. Thomas was thrust into the prison of the common thieves. But when the bishop saw that many were impressed by his example, and especially by his fastings and prayers (which things are deemed simple impossibilities amongst them), he removed him from his diocese, as if he were a pest, and remanded him to London, where to this day he perseveres in prison, to the great consolation and edification of many.

"One thing alone remains, which seems to afford a specimen of his great and unmeasured zeal, that from the time of his apprehension, and the consequent loss of all hope of going to Rome, he laboured all the more; and for the greater glory of God and the salvation of his neighbour, would have entered the Priesthood, but the great want of Bishops in England rendered this impracticable. How great affliction this caused him is known only to those who were intimate with him, and the more so because he saw that his want of Holy Orders hindered his doing much that he could otherwise have undertaken.

"But to return to the point; the only relief for this his twofold grief, and affliction of soul, is that your Paternity will be pleased to give him your fatherly consent to this his petition, to regard his sighs, his prayers and desires, now for these four years daily poured out before God, and would persuade yourself (which is most true) that Thomas Pounde has been so disposed towards the Society for the past seven years, that he would esteem all labours light to him were he but admitted to it.

"Indeed, I do not hesitate to affirm that he eagerly desires this favour of your Paternity for no other cause than that, fortified by our spiritual helps, and relying on the name and opinion of the Society, he may be able to effect greater good for his neighbours' salvation, which he daily yearns after with the whole affection of his heart.

"In the Roman College, 4th November, 1578.

"Praise be to Almighty God, and to His Blessed Virgin Mother.

"Your Reverence's unworthy son in Christ,

"Thomas Stephens."

Father General accordingly admitted him on the 1st of December, 1578, and sent him the anxiously expected announcement by the following letter. He was then in the Tower.

"'Thomas Stephens, our very dear brother in Christ, relates many things to us of your constant piety and faith, which are most grateful to us, but especially that you have now for many years aspired with great desire to our Society. Therefore, although our Institute rules that we admit no one amongst our members unless he hath been well proved by many trials, yet nevertheless, moved by the very clear testimony, both of Stephens and others, and accepting as a long probation your labours and sufferings of so many years, we are induced to yield to your pious desires.

"Wherefore, by virtue of that authority which God our Lord hath deigned to bestow upon us, though unworthy, we now already embrace you as a son and brother, we receive and admit you to our Society, and as a true member engrafted into the whole body, and we do also at the same time make you a sharer and participant in all our works, our labours, and our merits. But we hope the mercy and infinite goodness of God will at some future time be so propitious to you, that as we greatly desire, delivered from these troubles, we may be permitted to enjoy your company and presence: but should the providence of God for any cause deprive us of this opportunity, we nevertheless wish that this thought should console you, that, after a few days of this brief life, we shall be so united together in that eternal immortality (which we should all look forward to, and keep before our eyes), that nothing may be able then to separate us.

"As for the rest, although I know that your virtue, which I hear is truly worthy of a Christian man, requires no confirmation, yet as a most dear son, I will briefly admonish you in the words of the Apostle, that you may be mindful to be a spectacle to God, to Angels, and to men; to God indeed as the bestower of eternal rewards for the smallest labours; to Angels as strengthened by their presence; to men also that you may greatly inflame them, as hitherto you have done by your example, to true piety, and to encourage such as need it to undergo dangers with alacrity for Christ. Which thing, however, we wish may be so prudently and cautiously conducted by you, that you neither run into open danger without cause and fruit —a course which is held to be, not courage, but rashness—nor that you destroy your health and strength by immoderate abstinence and fastings, to which we hear you are abundantly addicted; but rather, as the Prophet saith, that you take care to preserve your strength for God—*fortitudinem suam ad Deum custodire.*

"May our Lord, however, to Whom it always belongs to protect and defend innocence and integrity, especially when brought into any danger in His own cause, be so propitious to you, that He may either totally drive away from you all these troubles, or, should He deem it to be more expedient for you otherwise, may He increase in you fortitude, constancy, and salutary patience to endure them. At least we never cease, both ourselves, as also all of ours, to pray and beseech our Lord in this behalf. This one thing, however, I greatly desire of you, that you publish to no one this your determination regarding our Society, neither by habit or dress, nor by discourse, but that you keep your secret to yourself until better times beam forth, when this your desire, by the grace of God, may be openly followed out.

"In the meantime may the grace of Christ and the communion of the Holy Spirit be always with you.

"Rome, 1st December, 1578."

Father Bartoli mentions another letter of Father General written to Pounde, dated 15th April, 1580, exhorting him to renew his fervour, and reminding him that, being now a member of the Society of Jesus, he must never cease from the following of

Jesus with the Cross on his shoulders, however steep and difficult the way, even to the summit of Calvary, there to die with Him upon the Cross. His Paternity again cautions him whilst in England, and especially in the prisons, not to appear in the habit of the Society, as the times and place were unsuitable, but by sanctity of life, and despising of the world, to show that he no longer belonged to earth.

The following copy has been taken from one in the Archives de l'Etat, Brussels.* It does not, however, appear to contain any mention of the habit of the Society.

"To Thomas Pounde, in prison in England,—I could not omit so good an opportunity as now presents itself, of giving some answer to your letter, to salute you in our Lord, and for our mutual consolation, by this means of correspondence, seeing that no other is open to us. I hope you will receive no little joy in our Lord from the visit of this our common friend, who is the bearer of this letter to you, who will moreover give you a proof of my affection towards you, and with how great love we embrace you in the bowels of Christ.

"Now, although I know that you are abundantly stout-hearted, yet would I desire to exhort you in Christ, not only patiently, but with alacrity, to endure those troubles wherewith, for so long a time, by the

* *Collectio Cardwelli*, MSS. (S.J.), ex Arch. Belgico Bruxell, vol. i., p. 35 (1872, Stonyhurst).

permission of the Divine Goodness, you have been visited, so long as it shall seem good to the same Lord, that they continue. And that you will apply this saying of the Apostle St. James to yourself—'Let us esteem it as all joy when we fall into divers temptations, that our faith may become more precious than gold tried by the fire.' Of which truth so many illustrious examples are left us both by the holy Martyrs, as by the Head of Martyrs Himself, Jesus, of Whom we, since by His infinite kindness we are called to His companionship, ought to esteem it a great, truly the greatest of all favours, should He be pleased to admit us to the fellowship, as of other virtues, so also of that of His Cross; for whosoever will be a companion of His Cross, will likewise be of the glory of His rewards and immortality.

"I thought with this to salute you, at the same time also commending myself to your prayers. May our Lord Jesus be always with you, and vouchsafe to bless and prosper you in all things. Amen.

"Rome, 15th April, 1580."

Indescribable was the consolation of spirit in this holy cavalier of Christ, on receiving so great a favour, for which he had for so many years sighed. But at the same time his beloved Stephens had obtained another for himself in Rome; such an one that, to speak truly, says Father Bartoli, one knows not which of these two fortunate Englishmen most to envy in the lots fallen upon them from Heaven:

Pounde his thirty years of imprisonment for the confession of the faith; or Stephens his forty years' labour for the propagation of the faith. Father Thomas Stephens was the first of our English members to beg with many entreaties of Father General Mercurianus, and before applying to his Paternity, to seek from God with many tears and much penance, the favour of being sent out to the East Indies.

Having completed his course of philosophy, he was sent there, and arrived at Goa, after a six months' voyage, in September, 1580. There he commenced cultivating and increasing the small Christian community of Salsette, a peninsula near Goa. He was very near fructifying it with his blood, instead of his sweat, and sharing the fate of Father Ralph Acquaviva, and four others of the Society, who, two years later on, were martyred by the barbarous idolators in divers ways, in the same place, out of mere hatred of the faith. But it pleased God, for His own ends, to change for Stephens the short death by the sword for a long and hard apostolical labour of forty years, the space of time he spent in that onerous mission. So dear was he to the inhabitants, and so content to spend all his labours for the good of their souls, that he never asked for any better condition, nor for any change of place, neither did his Superiors venture, even for ever so short a space, to deprive Salsette of so profitable a labourer. He attained so great perfection in the Canary language, in use there, that he composed and published a grammar of it. He afterwards wrote another of the Hindostanee language, which is a more refined one, and in use amongst the higher classes; this was a more accomplished work. In each language he composed and printed such useful books upon faith and Christian piety, that on festivals, after Mass, they always read them to the Catholics. He died full of years and merits at Goa, in 1619, in the seventieth year of his age, mourned and wept over by his dear Canarians out of the love they bore him as a Father, and his indefatigable care of their souls as an Apostle.

Let us now return to the object of this notice whose wonderful life may be said to have been a continual martyrdom of thirty years, rendered all the more bitter to him, inasmuch as he more ardently desired to end it at Tyburn, to which passage, indeed, he was a hundred times within an ace of arriving; but he was not destined to reach the goal by that last and noble course. But as they used to say of him, if martyrdom was wanting to him, he was not therefore wanting to martyrdom.

After their remand from Winchester to London, Pounde and his companions were divided amongst different prisons. He wrote several times to them. The following is one of the letters.

"I am very often questioned by Mr. Young. I have twice been examined before five or six commissioners. Once I was brought out before a great assembly of persons, loaded with fetters. And because I was thought to stand up for the truth more freely before those who did not wish to hear it, I was then remanded to Newgate. The gaoler, as though I was already a condemned criminal, tore off both my hat and cloak; but what was equally a source of regret to him, as it was to myself, he left my head safe upon my shoulders.* As I went along with uncovered head, and heavily ironed, the mob cried out *Crucifige*—'Crucify him.' They liberally bestowed upon me the alms of the 'widow of Newgate' (a certain kind of instrument of torture called the 'widow's mite'). I awaited the sentence of the judges from four o'clock till the afternoon, when I was suddenly summoned. My manacles and chains were taken off, and my hat and cloak restored. I was conducted to Lincoln's [Inn] hall (where I formerly lived when studying the law) here; five commissioners here waited for me, and amongst them was Topcliffe, the prefect of the examinations.

"They had it in command from the Queen to recall me from my course of life, either by threats or by blandishments; but all was in vain. They urged upon me that, if I would prove myself faithful to the Queen and her loving subject, it was necessary that I should disclose the names of those with whom I was accustomed to consort, and the places of resort.

* Pounde never seems to have lost his natural playfulness of humour, in spite of all his great sufferings. We shall meet with several instances of it in the course of this narrative.

I replied that I was ready to make oath both of my own, and of the fidelity of all of them. As to the rest, it was not the part of a good man and a Catholic, and one of my rank and education, and having regard also to conscience, to bring innocent and friendly men into danger by disclosing their names. Finding that they could gain nothing from me by their coaxing words, they remanded me back to my prison. After two days, Topcliffe (that most unrelenting persecutor of Catholics) came to me with the governor of the prison. They endeavoured to shake my constancy by every kind of means; but they accomplished nothing; they deplore my condition; this specially grieves them—but in which I greatly glory—the faith, and my imprisonment for the faith's sake.

"After they were departed came Young again, who asked me what Topcliffe had been doing with me? The man (truly urban and affable!) feared lest Topcliffe, severe and rough as he was, should have done anything rude towards me.

"With the most winning manner of voice, he endeavoured to coax me to betray my friends, and to disclose any secret which might, perhaps, serve his wicked ends. Finding that he could gain nothing from me, he urged me to write a letter to the Lord Chancellor, asking for favour. I did so, indeed, but in such a manner that they could get no handle against me, and with such effect that from thenceforth they cared less about me, deeming me an obstinate fellow, and of all Catholics the most dangerous to the public safety of the realm—that is, the most hostile to heresy. Therefore here I am, secluded from the company of all the rest, without hope of a freer custody, unless by chance I am summoned again to the next sessions of Newgate, to answer the charge of my duty to God and defence of the Catholic faith. This I have to warn you of, O my companions in chains! that you believe not any sinister reports about me; and I would exhort you, with all my heart, to that perseverance in the faith I desire for you. Farewell!"

The evils of the prisons did not consist so much in their wretched condition, as in the brutal and coarse manners of the gaolers, who were either Protestants or Puritans. However, the Queen's Ministers utterly failed to weaken his courage by the insufferable punishments inflicted upon him, nor could they subdue him by the force of torments and pain: nay, he rather rejoiced in them, gaining thereby additional strength of heart; and frequently the example of his invincible courage would produce good effects even amongst Protestants, who to the shame of their own sect, had far to search ere they could meet with instances of such great virtue; whilst others could not refuse to their own eyes admiration of the virtue of Catholics, and this would soon after lead them to their own salutary repentance. Nor could their theologians, whether Protestant or Puritan, adduce against him any efficacious argument for his conviction and subversion. Indeed, he rather gave them so much to do, one while with his answers, another with his questions, that after the first attack, they would return no more to engage with him; and yet he had only gone as far as poetry and rhetoric in the academies, and the study of civil law; but from the excellency of his wit, his long and continuous study of the Holy Scriptures, the Fathers of the Church, and the principal articles of controversy between Catholics and Protestants, to which we may add his converse with Priests and learned Catholics in the various prisons in which he was confined, especially in those of Wisbeach and London, with Father William Weston, of whom Pounde says in a letter of the 3rd of June, 1609—"I was then his pupil in the Castle of Wisbeach, and afterwards, as far as I was able, a consoler in that of London." He had thus rendered himself not only impregnable, but terrible to his foes. And to their cost, two Protestant doctors of divinity, Tripp and Crowley, proved this. This was in September, 1580, Thomas being then in the Marshalsea prison, London. These two doctors, then, entered the prison to dispute with Pounde upon points of religion; they commenced, as these men are all accustomed to do with Catholics, with a storm of insult and abuse, most unbecoming towards such a distinguished man as Pounde was. He by his greatness of soul was no more moved than if he had heard the ravings of two madmen;

he took hold of a passage of Holy Scripture that one of them had quoted, and was badly interpreted to suit his own caprice. Upon this passage, Thomas raised a fundamental question as a necessary basis of the truth, because otherwise unless there is agreement in the definition, to determine upon it would only be to commence with words and end in smoke; so is it necessary to meet those that differ in the principles from which the conclusions are to be drawn. The point was—"Is Holy Scripture to be understood according to the private opinion of whosoever desires to be its expounder, or rather according to the universal and received understanding and mind of the Fathers of the Church?" No question more ungrateful could have been asked of the adversaries, because where they cannot make the Word of God speak according to their own will, there is an end of it; but since one can do it, another can also, and so each one, which is, finally, as much as to say that every man may make for himself a rule of faith; but which rule should be as much one, as the truth is one, and as infallible as the Word of God itself, and which consequently cannot disagree in interpreting the same passage contrary ways. That this happens to those who usurp to themselves this prerogative, it suffices to adduce the syllable *Est*, one of the words used in the consecration in the Divine Sacrifice, which is understood in a particular and private sense in no less than five different ways, each forming a different heresy. Therefore Luther was obliged to say that he had contended with thirty heresiarchs generated by the same liberty of making their private judgments the exponent of the mind of God; the which liberty he had adopted for himself, late to his grief, because others had appropriated it to themselves, and which was the origin of his going at last to the other extreme, saying—The *Bucolic* of Virgil could not be understood by any one who had not been for five years a shepherd; the *Epistles* of Cicero by any one who had not for twenty years governed a republic; the Holy Scriptures by any one who had not governed the entire Church, attended by Elias, Eliseus, John the Baptist, and the Apostles of the Redeemer, and finished with in part that of the poet Stasius—

> Hanc tu divinam ne Æneida tenta,
> —sed vestigia pronus adora.*

Now the two assailants of Pounde fared so badly, that at last, the more they had spoken, the less did they understand what they had said, and they thought it good luck to take themselves off with a short statement in writing of six reasons† that Pounde had given them in support of the argument sustained by him; to which he begged them for an answer, and for leave to reply should anything else occur to his mind.

* Bartoli, *Inghil.*, l. i., p. 127, vol. i.
† To prevent interruption in this narrative, a copy of the six reasons will be given in the second part. This dispute dates in September, 1580.

But these brave masters of Israel having read what was in the paper, and seeing that their reputation was placed in great jeopardy by having to answer in writing rather than orally, they betook themselves with the document to make a great noise to John Elmer, or Aylmer, the pseudo-bishop. They strove in his presence to make Pounde appear all the more ostentatious, because he not only refused to become Calvinist by their exhortations, but was all the more eager to publish in his own defence against them, treatises and writings of pestilential doctrine, as appeared in that paper which had just then issued from his pen, and which they then and there presented to the bishop.

Nothing further was wanting to put his lordship in a rage; for by his furious nature he was a very firebrand with every one, and his false zeal rendered him terrible as thunder to the Catholics. He remanded Thomas off hand from London to be immured in a prison far away. This was Storford, or Bishops-Stortford Castle, Herts, thirty miles from London, on the confines of Essex and Cambridge; a lonely place and well chosen. He was thrust into a cell a few feet under ground, in which was perpetual night, no ray of the sun nor any gleam of light ever entering there, whereby to distinguish between day and night. No one was allowed to visit him, for wherever this was allowed, he would gain many to the Catholic faith. The bare and dirty ground was his bed; a pair of heavy fetters were put on his legs, and handcuffs on his wrists, and chains. To these many other sufferings were added by his brutal gaoler.*

As the blacksmith was about to rivet the shackles upon his legs, Thomas endeavoured to kiss them, whereupon the smith inhumanly struck him with them upon his head, and drew blood; but he with a calm countenance said—"Would that blood might here flow from the inmost veins of my heart for the cause for which I suffer." The blacksmith was astonished at his words and patience under so great and so unprovoked an injury. And it pleased God, in reward of the merit of that patience, to give Thomas that soul, causing the smith to demand of him whence he possessed so great a confidence that he was of the true religion, seeing that in England "papist" and "reprobate" were synonymous terms.

* Bishops-Stortford was then an ancient half ruined castle of the Bishops of London. It was then used as a prison by them. Gorton, *Topogr. Dict.*, title Bishops-Stortford, says it was last used as such "by the execrable Bishop Bonner." Father Tanner, Father More, and Father Bartoli, borrowing from each other, are mistaken in treating this conference as taking place *after* Thomas had been half a year at Bishops-Stortford. Father Tanner says—"After half a year's confinement in the dark cells of Storford Castle, the authorities hoping thereby to have weakened the light of faith in him, remanded him back to London, to endeavour totally to extinguish it." The letters and papers procured from the State Papers in the Public Record Office, which are copied in the second part of this notice, clearly show the disputation to have been *before*, and in fact the cause of his being remanded to Bishops-Stortford. Those historians had then, probably, no certain data to guide them.

Thomas gave the man such strong reasons and convincing proofs, that he was vanquished, and afterwards became a Catholic, and in punishment for it was cast into prison, where he died piously in chains—*tanti est constantiam in asperis tueri.*

Whilst thus buried under ground, unseen and unheard of among the living, his two adversaries, Tripp and Crowley, went about boasting in public how they had vanquished him, and published a book in answer to his six reasons, if indeed that can be called an answer which avoids all mention whatever of the main point in dispute, and only charges him with an abominable calumny, saying that Thomas Pounde, the Papist, defended by word and writing the doctrine that the opinions of men were to be held in greater account than the Word of God expressed in the Holy Scriptures; thus giving a totally different colour to the good meaning he had expressed, viz., that the Holy Scriptures were to be understood, not by man's own private judgment (as the Puritans boast to have been privileged to do by the Holy Spirit), but according to the received and concordant opinion of the Fathers.

After half a year's confinement in the dungeons of Bishops-Stortford Castle,* the Bishop Aylmer removed him to Wisbeach Castle, whence, soon after, by an order of the Privy Council, the bishop remanded him to the Tower, for the purpose of

---

* See Thomas' letter to Sir Christopher Hatton, Sept. 18, 1580. Part second, p. 126, post.

F

being jointly examined with Father Campion, as we shall see in the second part of this narrative. The Lords wrote to Aylmer with this order in the month of August, 1581.

Father Henry More recounts various prisons in which Pounde was confined, but without giving dates, which probably he was unable to do. He says—"After one year" (probably in Newgate), "Pounde was removed to the Marshalsea Prison; thence he was thrust into the Tower of London; then transferred to the Compter on the other side of the Thames; thence to Wisbeach, a fortress at the head of the Isle of Ely, where for ten years he dwelt with many Priests and laymen, and most familiarly with Father William Weston. In the year 1597, he was again sent to the Tower; then to the Compter within the City; after that to the White Lion; then to the Gate-house, Westminster; afterwards to the Fleet Prison; and lastly, to Framlingham Castle, from whence he was liberated on bail by James I."

Father Thomas Stephens, who received it from Pounde, thus sums them up—"He was seven years in the Tower of London; four in the Marshalsea; half a year in Storford Castle; ten years in Wisbeach Castle; three years in Framlingham Castle; and the rest, to the number of thirty years altogether, in the various other places named."

Father Tanner says that when confined at Wisbeach his life was preserved by a singular interposition of

Divine Providence. He was sitting with the others at table, when a piece of the ancient ornamental ceiling, in which was a hollow place [and where probably they secreted sacred things], fell by its own weight, and must have crushed Thomas, had not its progress been suspended; and this was looked upon as not happening by chance, because just so much of the falling ceiling affixed to the wall as was necessary, remained hanging in the air over him, covering him like an umbrella, and he experienced no injury, "some holy things being kept in it."

Father Bartoli describes Wisbeach, where he says Pounde was left to rot alive for ten years, as a famous castle, and worthily so, for its horrid dungeons, and the blessed company of so many Priests and most noble confessors of the faith, sent there to rot in that foul atmosphere and stinking and marshy spot. For Wisbeach is a castle in the Isle of Ely (an inland island formed by the waters of various rivers that wash the extremity of the county of Cambridge from the north, between Lincoln and Norfolk). There the ground is so low that it cannot let off all the water of the many streams running into it; thus for want of an outlet, the water for a large extent within becomes stagnant and brackish. A creek of the sea which runs up there, also frequently breaks in and increases the evil. The prisons are rather one ruin than stone buildings; a palace near Wisbeach, a most antique place, and for a long time abandoned and forgotten, only that it occurred to the recollection of the Ministers of Queen Elizabeth to prepare it in their humanity, as a fitting place to cause by its pestilential air the deaths of the more saintly Catholics, to slay whom by the rope and the sword would be too manifest an exposure of their infamous injustice.* Wisbeach Castle, which had been selected in 1572, on account of its solitary site, as a place where the chief recusants should be imprisoned, and made "to live at their own charges," was now made the prison for such of "the capital Doctors and Priests" as were found "busier in matters of State than was meet for the quiet of the realm." Sir Nicholas Bacon was appointed keeper, and Michael and Carleton, the latter a sour Puritan, were to be the resident superintendents. Other places were apportioned for the other parts of England, to receive the recusants. The instructions to the keeper of Wisbeach Castle, which served for all the rest, required that, besides the usual rules of close confinement, a minister was to be appointed, to have "his charge of diet and other necessaries by the contributions of the recusants;" and the keeper was to see "that due exercise of common prayer be observed every day, and preaching twice in the week at least." At this the prisoners were to be present, or if they refused, they were to be fined at the pleasure of the Bishop of Ely. Each prisoner, moreover, was to be "twice conferred with

* Bartoli, *Inghil.*, l. i., cap. xv., p. 123.

in the week at least, as well by the minister as by other learned men sent by the bishop or that voluntarily of themselves should come for so charitable a work." But the prisoners were to have no conference with each other but at meal time, and then there was to be "no speech of any matters in controversy." Those who conferred with the minister were to have more liberty than those who did not. But none were to be allowed to have any books except a Bible, the works of the Fathers, and books licensed by the minister.

Nicholas Sanders, *De Schismate*, l. iii., gives a letter by a Priest from London to Father Agazzari, Rector of the English College, Rome, which states (*inter alia*) —" No access is allowed, and we are obliged to use tricks to communicate with them. When any one wants to give them an alms, he walks in the neighbouring fields the day before, and cries out as if he were looking for game.

"At this sign, one of them looks out of the window, and learns by signal that there is something for the prisoners. The next night, when every body is asleep, the sportsman cautiously creeps up to the wall, and one of the prisoners lets down a basket from the window whence the sign was given, and draws up what is put into it. The same plan is generally adopted for the other prisoners; but the variety of places requires a variety of methods, and the zeal, charity, and bravery of the Catholics is greatly conspicuous in designing and accomplishing these dangerous services."* (See Simpson's *Campion*, pp. 165, 166.)

* Thomas Pounde's name occurs in several of the State Papers in the Public Record Office.

1586. *Domestic, Eliz.*, State Papers, Vol. cxc., No. 44. "Names of prisoners at Wisbeach—Recusants, Mr. Scrope, Mr. Parpoint, Mr. Pounde." There were then eighteen Priests, including Fathers Weston, Mettam, Strange, and Bickley (not then S.J.). There appears to be some misdate in this, or in the letter of Younge next mentioned; Mr. Younge dates 1587, and says that Pounde was then in the White Lion Prison: the confusion may arise in the style.

1587. *Dom. Eliz.*, Vol. cciii., No. 20. Letter from Mr. Richard Younge to Walsingham. He says (*inter alia*), "Whereas your honor thinketh it convenient that some should be sente to Wisbeach; it is most assured that lying here in London at libertie in the prisons, they doe much harm to such as resorte unto them; especially William Wigges, George Hide, and George Collinson, Priests, prisoners in Newgate; Morris Williams, an old Priest, prisoner in the Clink, and *Thomas Pounde*, prisoner in the White Lion, taken as a layman, but (as Tirrell assureth me) he is a professed Jesuite, and was admitted by one substituted by Parsons while the said Pounde was prisoner in the Tower. These are most busy and dangerous persons, and such as in no wise are worthie of libertie, neither are they within the compass of the last statute; so that if your honor thinke so good, Wisbeach were a convenient place for them. There are so many others which will appeare to be of the same sorte, but for so much as *these* are principal malefactors, and that perhaps they be a number sufficient to be carried thither at one tyme. I will forbear to speake of the others until I shall deliver all their examinations."

Dom. Eliz., State Papers, Vol. cxcv., No. 115; Vol. cci., No. 53. "The names of divers persons certified to be receivers of Jesuites and Seminaries." The name of Thomas Pounde is added at the end, apparently in another handwriting, although he was at that time in prison.

160$\frac{2}{3}$. *Dom., Jac. I.*, Vol. vii., No. 50. List endorsed by Cecil—"A note of the Jesuits that lurk in England. In Framingham [amongst others] Mr. Pounde, a lay Jesuit."

Nor was Pounde at any time alone in these persecutions and troubles. The Catholics generally underwent equal vexation. For although his zeal in professing his faith made him appear more prominent in expressing his opinions and in defence of the Catholic cause than others (as an instance, it once happened that, observing a Priest hesitating before the judges at the question whether the Pope or the Queen should possess supreme power in England in matters ecclesiastical, and in danger of implicating himself by an evasive answer, Pounde openly called out to him, "Say the Pope, for to whom else does the right better belong?" although to profess this was a capital offence), nevertheless the interests of all classes of men were banded together for the ruin of the Catholics; so that each one, *in suo foro*, urged on by every effort and diligence the extirpation (if by any means it were possible) of the orthodox faith.

Father Parsons, in a letter dated 17th November, 1580, to the Rector of the English College, Rome, thus mentions these miserable times*—"The heat of the persecution is most violent, and such as hath not been since the very constitution of England. The noble, ignoble, men, women, and even children, are dragged off to the prisons; bound in iron fetters, deprived of the light of day, plundered of their property, and as well by public edicts as by speeches and sermons, defamed before the common people as

---

* More, *Hist.*, l. ii., n. xxi., p. 52.

traitors and rebels! In these past months many men of rank, respectabilty, and wealth, and whoever possesses influence in his own neighbourhood, have been confined in the prisons; and to such an extent that not only are the old prisons of England, but even many new ones that have been built, insufficient to receive the Catholics; and yet pursuivants are despatched in quest of others, indeed the number of them, *per Dei gratiam*, so daily increases, that the persecutors themselves are well nigh tired out; and indeed all this is pretended to the common people as done for the good of the commonwealth; but in reality religion is attacked."

Nor did Pounde experience at the hands of the judges more justice than he had received from the veritable masters of the truth amongst the Protestants. Norton,[*] one of the assessors or advisers of Hopton, the superintendent of the Tower, and of the slaughter of Priests and Catholics incarcerated there, tried to persuade him, as a means of getting rid of Pounde, and thus saving the honour of their sect, which he both by living and speaking overturned, to declare him mad, and as a madman, to consign him to the infamy and beatings of Bedlam, the London asylum of the violent and insane. There is no record that this wicked advice was acted on; but it is related of the wife of this brutal assessor, that a little while after, she herself became mad, and was confined in the same Bedlam; as a just punishment of God

[*] He was the rack-master of the Tower.

receiving the very same treatment that her husband had, in the face of all justice, designed for Pounde!

Out of a large number of cases of oppression of this sort, Father Bartoli selects the following, which occurred in the last year of Pounde's imprisonment.

Two innocent Catholics, in the county of Lancaster, had been condemned to death by the judges, and had been executed accordingly. To go into particulars of their case would be both a long history and irrelevant to our present narrative. One of these men (it is hardly credible) was cut down before he was half dead, and quartered alive; the other was hung till dead.

The judicial process, the guilt of the accused being presumed, but not proved, was so flagrantly contrary to all law, both natural and statute, that the lives of Catholics seemed to have arrived at the lowest estimate, even as that of brute animals, which their owners slaughter at their will, how and when they please.

James of Scotland had a few months before arrived in England, having succeeded to the crown, to which he was heir, on the death of Elizabeth, which happened 24th March, $160\frac{2}{3}$, and to judge of him according to all appearances up to that time, no one could have imagined that he would be so evilly disposed towards Catholics, but that such a wilful slaughter would have displeased him, and that by punishing the iniquity of these judges he would have made an example to deter others, and thus diminish the persecution of the Catholics, which was caused in great part by the hatred of the Protestant ministers. Impressed with this pious, just, and prudent idea, our Pounde drew up, at his own instance, a solemn charge against the iniquitous judgment passed upon the two Catholics at Lancaster, and sent it for presentation to the King. Whether it ever came to hand or not, Pounde was summoned for trial in the court called the Star Chamber, at Westminster, in which court criminals of great note, slanderers, cheats, and similar grave offences are tried.

Here, therefore, he was summoned to be convicted and condemned as a calumniator of the judges of Lancaster before the King. So this court supported the summons of the judges, and proved the fact, that to ruin the Catholics, there was no difference between one tribunal and another.

This trial lasted for eight hours. It occurred 29th November, 160$\frac{3}{4}$, and more than one entire hour was consumed by the Attorney General in a severe invective against slanders, and slanderers, and finally against Thomas himself; in whose case, above all the other Catholics, he made a digression from the cause, to call to the remembrance of the court how it was their fault that Pius V. had fulminated his Bull against Elizabeth, to strip her of her crown; and other similar reminiscences rendering Catholics there most odious. He confronted Pounde, now transformed from an accuser into a criminal, and constrained him to reveal whence he came to know the nature of the Lancaster judgment, so far distant as it was from Southampton and from London?

Perhaps he had, throughout, accomplices and confederates by whose means he obtained his information; he must reveal, or they would compel him by torture; and as regarded the condemnation of the two Catholics at Lancaster, the skilful Attorney General affirmed that they were guilty, and that the sentence of the judges was most just; nor to prove it did it cost him more than his mere simple assertion, which passed for truth, equally as though it was the very fact. There were contained in that court three judges for passing sentence, viz., the Lord Chancellor, the Lord Treasurer, and the Lord Chief Justice, to which trio, as the highest in that dignity, was given the surname or style of "Great." Besides these there were Earls, Viscounts, Barons, and other minor officials, the usual number that assembled to form this the highest tribunal. Each one of these spoke in condemnation of Pounde. Whatever he said in his own defence was scornfully listened to; and in fine the Lord Chancellor, taking from the Lord Chief Justice the sentence, pronounced Thomas Pounde condemned in a fine of £1,000. Besides this, as a slanderer, his ears were to be cut off (his being a Catholic was sufficient to prevent his rank as a cavalier being any protection against his being punished as the vilest of rogues are). But, because (continued the Lord Chancellor) a man of that age (sixty-five years old) perhaps would not be able to survive the pain, instead of it let him be nailed by one of his ears to the public pillar of justice at Westminster; after so many hours let him be unfastened, and taken to Lancaster (a journey of several days) and there let him be nailed by the other ear to the public pillar of justice. This punishment corresponds (says Father Bartoli) with the pillory in Italy, except that there a collar of iron is used to fasten the criminals to that public place of shame, but in England it is done by a nail that pierces the ear, and by that means most effectually fastens the man to the pillar. There was added to the sentence that in both places an infamous mitre should be placed on his head, upon which should be inscribed his offence, which he could never be induced to confess himself.*

Thus sentenced he was remanded to prison, where, added the Lord Chancellor, if the fear of the imminent and certain evil about to befall him, shall bring him to a better mind, he is declared discharged from the infamy of the nailing by the ears; but if not, let

---

* The punishments awarded by the criminal code, in former times (and these not so far off from our own days), were verily both most excessive and barbarous, and ill-proportioned to the offences, forming a strange contrast with modern times. What would be thought now-a-days of the following—*Dom. Jac. I.*, Vol. 159, No. 70, 1624, February 22. Letter of Mr. Chamberlain to Dudley Carleton (*inter alia*). "*Moore, an attorney, for speaking ill of Queen Elizabeth and Henry VIII., was sentenced to lose both his ears, and to imprisonment during pleasure. He laughed whilst the sentence was performing in Cheapside.*"

him be kept in prison until he either dies, or reveals his accomplices in defending the cause of justice to Catholics. So far my Lord Chancellor!

It does not appear from any records that this infamous sentence was actually carried out. But this is beyond all doubt, that neither could the fear of it, nor of a thousand deaths, ever draw from the mouth of our noble confessor a word in prejudice of any Catholic whosoever he might be. His friends and relations, being advised of this shameful condemnation, in order to save him from it, employed the interest of the Spanish Ambassador, at whose entreaties the Queen asked the favour of the King; but both the one and the other received an angry reply, and were forbidden, in addition, ever again to interfere in the like matter, where religion was concerned, nor to intercede for any guilty Papist. And had not the Ambassadors of the King of France and the Doge of Venice, who were more successful in their exertions to soften the heart of King James towards the Catholics, by their united entreaties prevented the execution of the sentence, we have no assurance that it would not have been carried out, at least in part. It is certain that the sentence of imprisonment for life was respited.

A person who met with Pounde, in the same Star Chamber, and was present at that conviction, and wrote a full report, from which Father Bartoli says he has abridged his account, wisely cautions all, whoever they may be, to whom reports may be sent out of

England, against the credit to be given not only to the annals and histories of Stow, Hollingshead, Goodwin, and Camden, all of them Protestants (however great merit may be due to those authors for their great labours), when they represent the Catholics of England as guilty, *because* condemned, but to the acts of the trials themselves, presumed to be solemn and legal, of the criminal court, whether of London, the head court of the kingdom, or elsewhere; because, as appears by the proceedings themselves, it happens that at the sole will and ruling of the judges the Catholics are found guilty by the juries, while their adversaries are acquitted. This writer goes on to observe that, if here under the very eyes of the King himself, his own special tribunal so flagrantly violates its official power and the very name of justice, so wickedly inverting facts and their proofs, thus giving the semblance of truth to lies, and *vice versa* of falsehood and calumnies to truth, acquitting the guilty and condemning the innocent, what are we to expect from other tribunals of the kingdom, where causes of religion are in question, being as they are so much the less laid open to the complaints of the oppressed, as they are further removed from the ears of the King? Cases are not wanting where, on the Catholics being demanded by the clerk of arraigns the usual question—"Guilty or not guilty," would answer "Not guilty;" while the official would actually note down as the answer, "guilty;" and these would stand convicted as pleading "guilty," though not by their own act, but at the will of the Attorney General.

But to resume again the last acts of Pounde. If the generosity of his spirit, which never seemed to relax, or become less strong than at the first, under the continued redoubling of his sufferings and public ignominy of his thirty years' incarceration, is worthy of our admiration, much more is his great addition of voluntary self-inflicted austerities, loading his own beast of burthen (for so he used to call and to treat his body) with so heavy a weight, that it was necessary for our Very Reverend Father General to give him a loving reprehension, and to counsel him to reduce them to a more reasonable and supportable measure. But he was excusable, living as he did, from day to day as though he should die the next, and he had no notion at all of reserving himself for the time to come, but his only care was to multiply merits for the present hour; and he had good cause for this his daily expectation of death, since the fear of it never restrained him from openly professing, both in public and in his own examinations before the judges, in his private discourses, and in his writings upon the point, that Queen Elizabeth was not only not the head and governess of the Church in England, but that she had not a shadow even of spiritual jurisdiction above any other woman. Now to utter this, even *sotto voce*, being a mortal offence, and the sole cause to so many Catholics of a condemnation to a shameful death, had he not good reason continually to expect it, and to live each day as though the following one would bring it?

Many things, too, at this time were freely broached by the judges, particularly upon the subject of the Queen's supremacy in matters ecclesiastical which led him to form not a conjecture only, but a hope that, at the ensuing sessions at Newgate, he would be called upon to plead capitally. Therefore, as we have seen, figuring death as at the gate, he omitted no kind of pious practices, both to prepare himself for so happy an exit, as also to enkindle its desire by prayer, reading, and writing. He wrote at times not a few treatises, which were committed to memory by the diligence of Father Thomas Stephens, before named.

The principal were to prove the necessity of penitence, by four arguments—(1) from the great multitude of sinners; (2) the immense multitude of false prophets; (3) from the cruelty of the Turks and heretics; (4) from recent prodigies or omens in the skies and on earth. He subjoins remedies for all mortal sins. He then gives ten aids or consolations by way of self-incitements to undergo death with a ready courage. Because by death he should expiate for his own sins; and for the cause of God, and justice' sake, after the example of Christ, he should give up his life before he had seen either the overthrow of England (an event then generally foreboded), or the times of Antichrist; and he should thus, in whatever degree, be watering the seed of the faith with his own blood, and in however small a measure he should thus be rendering aid to the constancy of Catholics, the confusion of the heretics, and defence of religion. But for that short passage of death after which he so ardently sighed, was to be substituted his long-continued imprisonment.*

It is recorded of him that he took frequent and bloody disciplines, he slept little, and that with inconvenience, having no other bed for a long time than the bare and damp ground or soil of the prisons. He eat but once a day, which practice passed into a custom with him, which he never broke through for forty years, until at length old age obliged him to take a little collation in the evening. "Pardon me, your Reverence," he wrote from Belmont in an account of conscience to his Superior in England, "if I relate in confession my experience of so many years of my solitary life. Flying from the Court, I lived as a hermit for nearly seven years before I

---

* Among the flood of publications to which Father Campion's capture and execution gave rise, was one by Anthony Munday, London, 1582. "This called forth the following little book, edited, I think, by Pounde, for printing which Vallenger was condemned in the Star Chamber to lose his ears in the pillory. 'A true report of the death and martyrdom of Mr. Campion, Jesuite and Priest, and Mr. Sherwin, and Mr. Bryant, Priests, at Tiburne, the 1st December, 1581 : observed and written by a Catholic Priest, which was present thereat. Whereunto is annexed certain verses made by sundry persons.' 16mo, 26 leaves. The poets I take to be Henry Walpole, Pounde, and Vallenger himself" (*Vide* Mr. Simpson's valuable Appendix, *Life of Campion*, App. iv., nn. 6, 7, p. 350).

was imprisoned; these added to thirty years in prison, and the last three years since which I have not stirred abroad, reckon forty years; in which course of time I have proved that, after humility and poverty of spirit, the fervent love of God, and contempt of the world, there is no more terrible scourge to the devil than fasting, prayer, and watching."* As regards fasting he called it a strong fish-hook, wherewith to enable the fisher of souls in this kingdom to take a good haul.

His dress was neither a slovenly nor a cast-off one: on the contrary, it was rather a gay one, not for vanity's sake (God forbid), but by way of protest, that to a captive for the profession of the faith of Christ, and in constant expectation of being called out to die for it, every day was a solemn feast; and he would not that the adversaries, much less the Catholics, should imagine it to be a state of infelicity, and ignominy, but rather one of happiness and glory. Prayer, the study of the holy Fathers, writing controversy, and treatises against the current heresies and in defence of the Roman faith, and its reasons, and in treating of the affairs of the soul with his companions in prison, when he had any, was his method of spending the greater part of the night and the whole day. And that all this was not useless as regards others, who were assisted in heart by the example of his life and the powerful efficacy of his

* Letter of 3rd June, 1609, quoted by Father Bartoli, *Inghil.*, l. i., cap. xvii., p. 131.

words, it is proof sufficient to relate the rage of the bishop, who on being apprised of the transformation effected by Thomas in the prisons, converting them into churches, the heretics into Catholics, and of these, the tepid and wavering into fervent and courageous, they hunted him from their prisons, sending him to be buried in others far removed from their dioceses, solitary, and deserted by men, to the end that, as in the case of the affected with deadly poison, his touch and his breath should not poison others.

"Our Pounde," as Father Parsons writes of him,* "is separated far away from all the prisoners, he is most strictly guarded in a lonely castle, and made to stand there for the greater part of the time with a heavy weight of iron upon his back, in punishment of his having freely reproached, to their vexation, the evangelicals, so they call their preachers. To penetrate to him in prison is almost impossible, and to a great extent, most dangerous; and a Priest who secretly carried him the Blessed Sacrament, was surprised and imprisoned.

"Now, by God's mercy, the access is a little facilitated; so much so, that we send to him, and he in return to us, reciprocally, with letters and messages, and thus we get frequent accounts of his battles and contentions with the preachers. They

---

* From London, 16th June, 1581, to Very Reverend Father General Aquaviva, quoted by Father Bartoli, *Inghil.*, l. i., cap. xvii., p. 134.

say that his prison is as it were entirely buried under ground, and totally dark and gloomy; that he sees no other light than that of an oil lamp, and this anything but such an one as he would desire, nor can he ever procure a better by money or entreaty. He sleeps for the most part of the night on the damp ground, bound sometimes with one, two, and often with three iron fetters: nevertheless, he writes merrily to us, and as though he had nothing to say about his prison nor his sufferings."

In this manner of life did our glorious confessor arrive at the thirtieth year of his imprisonment, divided into ten stations, agreeing in number, as he himself says, to the ten prisons into which he was thrust.

It occurred at this time to King James to banish from the kingdom the Priests who had been captured, and who, according to the brutal laws of Elizabeth, were guilty of death, and entirely to liberate all laymen.

Hereupon Thomas was remanded to his paternal mansion at Belmont, which, as we have said, is twelve miles from Winchester. Some time after this the Privy Council granted him a written licence to cross the seas, "well knowing," as Pounde says in one of his letters, "that I had no other intention than to give myself up to the Society, and to throw myself at our Father's feet. And I had already prepared to break through every hindrance, and betake myself there, mindful of the last words spoken to me by Father Henry Garnet, which are also those of the Apostle whose spirit he had imbibed, *Non quærimus vestra, sed vos*—When, lo! an order came from the Superior whom I obey, and in whose hands I should be as a staff."

The remainder of this noble champion's life from his discharge out of prison till his death, a period of about eleven years, may be well inferred from the following letter he wrote to Father Parsons six years before his death. It shows the affection he always entertained towards the Society, and the foundations of virtues by which he preserved patience under persecution for so many years. This letter is given by Father More, *Hist. Prov. Angl.*, l. ii., n. xxii., p. 52.

"Great was my joy of soul when your letter of the 3rd of January was delivered to me, especially the greeting added by Father Claudius to me the least and most unworthy of his sons, for I had received no news from you for a long time. From that day, indeed, until the 15th of May, I remained uncertain what that meekest and humblest of men, my Superior, here willed concerning me.

"At length a letter from him has made this sufficiently known to me. But that the case is so, I say that I am greatly ashamed at my silence of so many years, and on my knees prostrate to the ground at the feet of both, I pray your indulgence. For neither have I met my Superior as I should have done, nor have I addressed your Reverence by letter, and I candidly confess that I find no door of excuse for my negligence. Your Reverence, however, will, perhaps, for the sake of blessed Edmund Campion, whose memory is in benediction, open your bowels of charity to me. Your Reverence loves him; I venerate him with all possible respect. However, not only in those letters, but in your books (which are a consolation to many in England, and a help to those abroad), I am so greatly lauded that, whether in hearing or reading them, I am completely put to the blush. I congratulate you much, Reverend Father, who like another Israel, are wrestling with God for the preservation and conversion of England. As to what regards myself (to whom our good and great God gives somewhat to suffer), I arrogate nought to myself, since nought I deserve.

"I subscribed my last letter to our Reverend Father General: *Tot annis in statera appensus, Thomas Pondus*—'So many years weighed in the balance.' If in that time or afterwards, anything was accomplished, the favour was of God, not my act. To you, my best of Fathers, I have written nothing. This I think may be ascribed to my timidity and pusillanimity. Indeed I blame my own negligence for not having shown any token either of kindness or of gratitude towards those whom I so greatly honour, and which honour how great it is, is patent to those to whom all things here are manifest. If you ask whence this pusillanimity and fear, I believe it arises from hindrance. For I was for the space of thirty years dragged through various prisons for the cause of Christ and the Gospel. At the commencement I was mulct in sixteen, afterwards in eighty golden crowns per month, and which I paid into the treasury (the whole amounting to twenty-one thousand one hundred and twenty crowns).*

"And lastly, when thinking of crossing the seas, having made over my estate to two nephews (who, being born of heretical parents, I have brought up and educated as Catholics, as though they were my own sons), and with one foot as it were on the vessel, I was ordered to desist by my Superior (to whose nod I conform myself, as the old man's staff) until our Very Reverend Father's, or your Reverence's determination should be known about me. Therefore, put off with hopes, and vainly hoping long against hope, tossed about with many storms and tempests, I nevertheless resolved, naked and poor, to offer myself, although late, as a fruitless and barren tree, that if by chance in this miserable cadence of my life, I can bring forth any fruit, it may be for your Reverence's merit and

---

* Father More mentions a case in which he was fined by the Bishop of Winchester sixteen thousand crowns for refusing to apostatize. "He had a good esquire's estate, but it was so plundered by fines and exactions, that even his enemies were ashamed of their cruelty. Yea, Salisbury himself upon my plaint, telling him that our Gospel taught out of Christ's own mouth, that it was more blessed to give than to take away, as they had taken so much from me, took so much compassion on me, for his own honour, as to give me back twenty pounds for my relief, of two hundred pounds, which from a ward that fell to me of one of my tenants, he had taken from me and given to his secretary."

consolation. Your Reverence, with your accustomed charity, asks me what I am doing? What progress I make in spirit, what fruit, what consolation in my adopted mode of life? To speak plainly as I think, I say well, and most happily, as I hope. For what I once said to my keepers when taken to Framlingham Castle, the same I repeat now, and shall I hope say as long as I live, *Hanc quam pro Societatis, toga gero vestem non regiâ coronâ commutarem*—'I would not change this habit of the Society which I wear, for the Queen's crown.'

"I live with my two nephews frugally indeed; for my means are not such as is commonly reputed, because, forsooth, I give more amongst the poor than my neighbours, I mean the rich; and, because I make little account of those things after which others so eagerly gape, the honester sort, for the most part, wish me well. After a refection at midday (which practice of abstinence I would were also familiar to fishers of souls), my supper in the evening consists of bread and cheese; my drink is beer. I interdict myself from wine and medicine. *Cibus est medicina valenti*—'Food is the medicine of the healthy.' For the last three years I have had much ado with my friends and domestics, for holding to my mode of life. However, I hold on my course, and will stick to it, trusting to the prayers of our Blessed Lady and the whole celestial court. *Non enim existimo me comprehendisse, sed ad destinatum persequor ad bravium supernæ vocationis*—'I count not myself to have apprehended, but this one thing I do, forgetting those things which are behind, and reaching forth unto those things that are before, I press forward towards the goal of my high vocation.

"Your Reverence assist me with your prayers, whose most unworthy son I am.

"THOMAS PONDUS.

" From my former house, at Belmont,
3rd July, 1609."

He lived nearly six years after this, viz., to the 5th of March, 1615, on which day God called him to the reward of his faithful service of so many years, and the great merits of his multiplied sufferings and labours. He died in the same room at Belmont, in which seventy-six years before he had given at the time of his birth, as before remarked, that auspicious augury of himself by lifting his arm first to his head, and then on high, in the manner of a conqueror. He was a man truly wonderful, who wearied out, as he wrote to another, so many judges, magistrates, and doctors, so furious and so set upon injuring him. But at last, despairing of success, they tortured him in his life, and plundered him of his property. Finally, seeing him utterly indifferent both as to the one and the other, in comparison of the faith and of his soul, in admiration of him, they changed their hatred into regard, and their contempt into reverence. "Therefore, both living and dead, his memory is most celebrated in that persecuted

Church; although it would have been intolerable pain to the modesty of that holy man, to see himself lauded by the writers of the time, and in the diaries in which his fellow-prisoners for the same cause of the faith registered day by day the events that happened to him and the others, especially in the celebrated Tower of London."*

* Bartoli, *Inghil.*, l. i., cap. xvii.

Part II.

We now proceed to the second part of this narrative, viz., Thomas Pounde's connection with Father Campion and Father Parsons in their evangelical labours, and with those times, his letters, &c. In doing so it will be necessary at some little length to go into the history of that exciting period.

Father Campion and Father Parsons arrived in England, and in London, on different days in the month of June, 1580. On arriving in London, Father Parsons went to the Marshalsea Prison, where he found our confessor, who received him with open arms, and introduced him to Mr. George Gilbert, a quondam convert of that Father, who bountifully provided for all his wants and comforts, as he did also for Father Campion on his arrival.*

Father Campion and Father Parsons finding London emptied of friends, and swarming with spies, which rendered further stay both useless and dangerous, they determined with the other Priests to go forth on their appointed missions into the shires. Each of the Fathers was furnished with two horses and a servant, two suits of apparel for travelling, sixty

* His Life forms the second part of this volume.

pounds in money, books, vestments, and everything needful for the church or for the road, by George Gilbert, who also promised to supply whatever more might be necessary for them. Gilbert was the founder and the soul of a young men's club, the object of which will be more fully stated in the Life of Mr. Gilbert. The members binding themselves to perform the two functions of preparing Protestants and the safe conduct of the Priests, besides procuring alms for the common fund, out of which the Priests were supported. Not only did their peculiar position force these young laymen into such an association, but the various difficulties of the missionary Priests made the cooperation of some such body absolutely necessary. The penal laws were already very severe, and held out strong inducements to the laymen to betray the missionaries. Prudence, therefore, forbade them to compromise themselves, or the persons whom they visited, before they knew that their visits would be safe to themselves or agreeable to the parties. For this reason our Fathers were ordered to be very careful whom they conversed with; on no account to have any personal dealings with any Protestant, until his Catholic friends had sounded his disposition, secured his impartiality, and learnt that the Priests might speak with him without fear of being betrayed. All this required an extensive organization among the Catholic gentry.

Further, as the safety of the Priests required that they should know to whom they were going to trust themselves, and should be protected and conducted on their way from house to house, so did the safety of the host require that he should know whom he was receiving. Priests could not carry about with them the certificates of their Priesthood, still less the proofs of their honesty. Unknown strangers might be spies, or false brethren, or fallen Priests, as easily as honest men. It was necessary then that the missionaries should be conducted by some well-known and trustworthy person; hence this conductor had to be a gentleman well known and respected throughout the country.

Such functions entailed upon these guides great sacrifices; they determined "to imitate the lives of the Apostles, and devote themselves wholly to the salvation of souls and conversion of heretics." They promised "to content themselves with food and clothing, and the bare necessaries of their state, and to bestow all the rest for the good of the Catholic cause." Their association was solemnly blessed by Pope Gregory XIII., 14th April, 1580.*

The members soon became known as "subseminaries;" "conductors, companions, and comforters of Priests;" "Lay-brothers," "lay assistants," to "straggle abroad and bring in game;" whose business it was "not to argue, but to pry in corners, to get men to entertain conference of the Priests, or inveigle youths to fly over sea to the Seminaries."

* Vide *Dom. Elizabeth*, State Papers, Vol. cxxxvii., No. 128, a copy of which has been obtained from the Record Office.

They entered on their dangerous and difficult path with "extraordinary joy and alacrity, every man offering himself, his person, his ability, his friends, and whatever God had lent him besides." George Gilbert was the first. The list includes some of the first Catholic families, the Vaux's, Throgmortons, Tichbournes, Abingdons, Fitzherberts, Stonors, &c. Among them must have been at one time Lord Oxford, Lord Henry Howard, Lord Paget, and Thomas Pounde. Equipped by these gentlemen, Father Parsons and Father Campion rode forth, the first accompanied by George Gilbert, the second by Gervase Pierrepoint. They agreed to meet and take leave of each other at Hogsdon [? Hoxton], at the house, probably, of Mr. Gardiner, Father Parsons' first convert.

Just before they left Hogsdon, Thomas Pounde, then a prisoner in the Marshalsea, but who had found means to blind his keeper to his temporary absence, came to them in great haste. He said that a meeting of associates, of the prisoners and others, had been held at the gaol to discuss the means of counteracting the rumours which the Privy Council was encouraging.

It was believed that the Jesuits had come into England for political purposes. This story, said Pounde, would grow during their absence from London and would gain fresh strength with every fresh report of the conversions which they were about to make in the shires; the Council would be exasperated, and should either of the Fathers ever fall into its hands, he would be guilefully put out of the way, or openly slaughtered, and then books would be published to misrepresent him, according to the usual fashion of the day; hereby well-meaning people would be deceived, and the Catholic cause not a little slandered. But much of this, he went on to declare, would be remedied if each of the Fathers would write a brief declaration of the true causes of his coming, and would leave it properly signed and sealed with some sure friends until the day he might be taken or put to death. And then, if the enemy should falsely defame him, his friends might publish the declaration to justify his memory before God and man. Hence Pounde begged both of them to write their declarations, as if they were writing their last will.

The proposition was accepted by both the Fathers. Father Parsons' paper is preserved among the Stonyhurst MSS. Father Campion rose from the company, took a pen and seated himself at the end of the table, where in less than half an hour he wrote the declaration which was soon to be so famous. It was written without preparation, and in the hurry of a journey; yet it was so "pithy in substance and style" that it was a triumph to one party, and poison to the other.*

As Thomas Pounde may really be looked upon as the originator of this famous challenge, it may not be

* See Mr. Simpson's *Campion*, pp. 156—9, and the authorities quoted by him in his valuable notes, &c.

out of the way to give the following copy of it, taken from the State Papers in the Public Record Office.* It is addressed to the Lords of the Privy Council, before whom Father Campion expected to be examined when he should be apprehended. The spelling has been somewhat modernized, the original being in some parts scarcely readable.

"✠ JESUS—MARIA, 1580.

"Most Hon.—Whereas I have come out of Germanie, and Boeme-lande, being sent by my Superiors, and adventured myselfe to this noble realme, my dear countrie, for the glorie of God and benefit of soules, I thought it likely enough that in this busie, watchfull, and suspicious worlde, I should either sooner or later be interrupted and stopped of my course. Wherefore, providinge all doubts and uncertainties, what may become of me when God shall haply deliver my body into durance, I supposed it needful to put this writinge in a readiness, desiring your good lordships to give it the readinge, and to knowe my cause. This doinge, I thinke I shall ease you of some labor, for that which otherwise you must have sought for by practice of witt, I doe lay now into your hands by plain confession. And to that intent, that this whole

* *Dom. Eliz.*, State Papers, Vol. cxlii., No. 20, 1580. It is the one sent up by the Sheriff of Wilts to the Council, with Pounde's six reasons, letters, &c., which will be given presently. The collection is endorsed—"Certain Papisticall reasons set down for the withdrawing of men to come to the church, sent from the Sheriff of Wilts."

matter may be conceived in order, and so the better both understood and remembered, I make hereof these nine points, or articles, directly, truly, and resolutely opening my full enterprise and purpose.

"I. I confesse that I am, albeit unworthie, a Priest of the Catholic Church, and, through the great mercie of God vowed now these viij. years into the religion of the Society of Jesus; and thereby have taken on me a speciall kind of warfare, under the banner of obedience, and eke resigned all my interest and possibilitie of wealth, honor, pleasure, and other worldlie felicitie.

"II. At the voice of our General Provost, which is to me a warrant from Heaven, and an order of Christe, I tooke my voyage from Prague to Rome, where our sayd Father is always resiate, and from Rome to Englande, as I might and would have done joyfully into anie part of Christendome, or Heathenesse, had I been thereto assigned.

"III. My charge is of free cost to preach the Gospell, to minister the Sacraments, to instruct the simple, to reforme sinners, to confute errors, and in brief to crie all *arma spiritualia** against foul vice, and proud ignorance wherewith manie of my deare countriemen are now abused.

* The writing is difficult to decipher. The words may be read *allarme spiritualle*, though the meaning is much the same.

"IV. I never had minde, and am strictlye forbidden by our Fathers that sente me, to deale in anie respectes with matters of State or policye of this realme, and those things which appertaine not to my vocation, and from which I doe gladly restrain and sequester my thoughts.

"V. I aske, to the glorie of God, with all humilitie and under your correction iij. sorts of indifferent and quiet audiences: the first before your Honours, wherein I will discourse of religion so far as it toucheth the commonweal and your nobilities: the seconde whereof I make more accompt before the doctors, the masters and chosen men of both Universities; wherein I undertake to avow the faith of our Catholic Church, by proofs invincible, Scriptures, Councils, Fathers, histories, naturall and morall reasons: the third before the lawyers spirituall and temporall; wherein I will justifie the sayde faith by the common wisdom of the lawes standing yet in force and practice.

"VI. I would be loathe to speake anie thing that might sounde of anie insolent bragg, or challenge, especially being now as a dead man to this worlde, and willing to cast my head under everie man's foote, and to kiss the ground they treade upon. Yet have I such a courage in advancing the majestie of Jesus my Kinge, and such affiance in His gracious favour, and such assurance in my quarrell, and my evidence so impregnable, that because I know perfectly that none of the Protestants, not all the

Protestants livinge, nor any sect of our adversaries (howsoever they face men downe in pulpits, and over-rule as in their kingdom of grammarians, and of unlearned ears) can maintaine their doctrine in disputation. I am to sue most humblie and instantlie for the combat with all and everie of them, and the most principall that may be founde; protesting that in this triall, the better furnished they come, the better they shall be to me.

"VII. And because it hath pleased God to enrich the Queen, my Sovereign Ladye, with noble gifts of nature, learninge, and princely education, I doe verilie trust that if Her Highness woulde vouchsafe her royall person, and good attention to such conference, as in the ij. part of my fifth article I have mentioned and requested, or to a few sermons which in her or your hearinge I am to vtter, such manifest and fair lights, by good methode and plain dealinge, may be cast uppon those controversies, that possibly her zeal of truth, and love of her people shall incline her noble grace to disfavor some proceedings hurtfull to the realme, and procure towards us oppressed more equity.

"VIII. Moreover, I doubt not but you, her honorable council, beinge of such wisdome, and drift in cases most important, when you shall have heard these questions of religion opened faithfully, which many times by our adversaries are huddled upp, and confounded, will see uppon what substantial grounds our Catholic faith is builded, and how feeble that side is which by sway of the time prevaileth against us; and soe at last for your own soules, and manie thousand soules that depende uppon your government, will discountenance error where it is bewrayed and hearken to those that wolde spend the best blood in their bodies for your salvation. Many innocent handes are lifted vpp to Heaven for you dailie, and hourlie, by those English students whose posteritie shall never die, which, beyond the seas, gathering virtue and sufficient knowledge for the purpose, are determined never to give you over, but either to win you to Heaven, or to die uppon your pikes. And touchinge our Societie, be it known vnto you, that we have made a league—all the Jesuites in the world, whose succession and multitude must overreach all the practices of Englande—cheerfully to carry the cross that God shall lay vppon us, and never to dispaire your recoverie, while we have a man left to enjoy your Tiborne, or to be racked with your torments, or to be consumed with your prisons. The expense is reckoned, the enterprise is begun; it is of God, it cannot be withstood. Soe it was first planted, soe it must be restored.

"IX. If these my offers be refused, and my endeavours can take no place, and I, having run thousands of miles to doe you good, shall be rewarded with rigour; I have no more to say but to recommend your case and mine to Almighty God, the searcher out of hearts, Who send us of His grace, and set us at accord before the day of payment, to the end we may at the last be friends in Heaven, where all injuries [? miseries] shall be forgotten." *

Father Campion wrote this paper in haste, as we have seen, and gave a copy of it to Pounde, keeping the original himself. He desired that it might not be published till there was necessity for so doing; but he forgot to seal it as had been proposed, and as the more cautious Father Parsons took care to do. Pounde, therefore, went back to prison and read it, and was so excited by it that, though he had no intention of imparting it to his friends, still less of giving them, or allowing them to take copies of it, he was resolved not to hide its light.

The Marshalsea, in Southwark, one of the chief prisons for recusant Catholics, already mentioned in the first part of this notice, was at that time infested by two Puritan ministers, Mr. Tripp and Mr. Crowley, our old friends (*Vide* p. 54, &c., *ante*), who, under the protection of the authorities, visited the poorer prisoners in their cells, and urged them to "abide some conference" with them, "offering, like vain men in angles, to the uncharitable vexation of the poor prisoners," that disputation which they obstinately refused to abide in public. Pounde then, bursting with the secret of Father Campion's

---

* Reference is made to this famous protest or challenge in the letters of Fathers Campion and Parsons, given in the Life of George Gilbert, which forms the second part of this volume.

challenge, which he carried in his bosom, was inspired by it himself to make his public challenge to Tripp and Crowley (as related in the first part, page 54, &c., *ante*), and to back it up on the 8th of September, 1580, with petitions to the Council and the Bishop of London. Much of which it will be seen closely follows the eighth article of Father Campion's paper.

*Petition to the Lords of the Privy Council.**

"To the Right Hon. the Lords of Her Majestie's Privy Council, by all the Catholics in England, with one consent, as far as a few may presume of the minds of all the rest.

"Right Hon.—Whereas, oure Catholicke Prelates and Pastours are, and long have been either in prisons put to silence, or else in banishment, and all their bookes (God knoweth of what feare) also forbidden, which at the first they were challenged to put out as though they had no learning on their side to alleage. Verily, if it may please your honors, this maketh many hundreds, yea, thousands I might say, the more suspect our adversaries of fainting in their defence of learning, if the learned on our side should be admitted to anye manner of encounter in open conference with them. Nevertheless, a certain show there is now made, no doubt, at their petition,

---

* Taken from the original copy in the Record Office, 1580, *Dom. Eliz.*, State Papers, Vol. cxlii., No. 20. Sent by the Sheriff of Wilts.

as if they mistrusted not their cause that way, in that they come of late, and urge us, the inferior sort of our side, here in our chambers within the prisons to abide some conference with them. But when was it ever hearde, if your wisdoms will consider of it, that truth having the time to support it, did ever flie the day light, and creepe into corners? Our Saviour thus answered for all true preachers' example, when He was asked of His doctrine, *Ego palam locutus sum mundo*, etc.—I have uttered my doctrine to the world openly; I have ever taught in the Synagogues, and in the Temple, where all the Jews frequent, and in angles I have used noe speech. Why asketh thou Me? sayth He; aske them which have openlie heard Me, what My doctrine hath been. This noble answer, indeed, did cost our sweet Saviour a blowe on the eare. Your honours' pardon, yet we crave upon our knees, for [? aid] in this cause, which is God's cause, and of so many thousands of innocent people in this lamentable time of famine, both of truth and virtue. We beg the same of Her Majestie and you with one common crie; and them, more boldly we require, that they will soe speake openlie vnto vs likewise, and not in corners, where, if themselves be convinced, yet their shame shall be covered, and the seducer never the sooner detected. But withall, our humble suite to your honours is, that they may not only speake in open places to us, but that our preachers may have free leave and license to speake in the same place as openly to them again. Without which equal permission it is most evident that by any close conference nothing less is sought for than the truth, but either some glorie to our adversaries without victory, or the discredit of us, to make us to be reported for obstinate and ignorant men, through their good tongues, whose envie at us, we are acquainted with. But if Her Majestie, whose princely uprightness, with zeal of truthe, love of her people, and of learninge also, we honour on our knees, will vouchsafe to proclaim her edict of free leave and license to anie of our side in prison or abroade, within or without the realm, to come before her royal presence, and to be permitted to open audience either by disputation, or by preaching interchangeably, which way soever our adversaries dare accept, no more but upon the honour of a prince's word, for our own assistants' safeties, whatsoever throwing of daggers, or shooting of daggers happen to them afterwards, as to the weaker side by malice of detected spirits, wherein God's will be done, seeing it is in zeal of souls, and for victory of truth. If, then, I say, there do not come forth before her Highness, either four to four, or six to six, within fortie days after to join the spiritual battle with them, yea, and that two or three of them shall challenge all their side to this combat, and give them leave to send to Geneva for Beza and all his brethren, to assist them, then do I the penner hereof for all our side, although most unworthie of that service, being, as I am, alreadie in your hands and mercie, I say I doe most willingly yield my head to you to be cut off, and my quarters to be set on London gates, at the forty days' ende. If our adversaries be afraid, as most certain it is they are, to come to such an open conference, then we humbly beseech your honours, let them not offer that here in angles, like vain men, to our uncharitable vexation, which not one but they doe obstinately refuse in open places against their owne salvation. But let this petition, made in the name of all the Catholicke fathers of our nation, remain for a perpetuall recorde and testimonie even to our enemies of our indifference, and of their insufficiencie. Muse not, my Lords, at this challenge, with a counterbuff, as the soldier saithe. For it is made in the further behalfe (as it may be presumed) of a perpetuall corporation and succession of moste learned Fathers, as anie without comparison in the world; with the aid of another good race besides, which cannot die, who have all vowed, as charitie hath inflamed them, either to win this realme again to the Catholicke faith, and that without any bloodshed, except their owne, at God's permission, or else to die all uppon the pikes of your sharpest laws, and win Heaven as they hope to themselves. The wisdome of God inspire your hearts, and preserve you everlastingly. The 10th of September, 1580.

"Your humble prisoner, prepared as I hope for weale and woe. "T. P."

"Two things there are, if it may please your honors, which have the more emboldened us to put up this petition to your honors, partlie because the parties which came to confer with us at the Marshalsea, did seem to like well of this waie, seeinge it was our suite which we stoode vpon, promising also to move it to the Bishop of London, for him to prefer it higher, and partlie for that the saide Bishop of London did answer Mr. Tripp, now at his telling him of it, that he himselfe had made the like suite to Her Majestie for manie years agone, and will doe it now again the rather if it be our desire; which answer doth bring us in credit to showe how farr the learned of our side are well knowne to be from disagreeing to such a triall."

" Oure letter to the Superintendent* of London.

"Most heartily wishinge your lordship all honor, with grace and peace indeede unfained. Understandinge, as we doe, that your side will not refuse a conference, as we have all made our humble petition, with one common crie to have admitted, we humbly beseech you not to suppress this our petition, when it shall come to your hands, but to prefer it up to the councill, to whom it is made, and that with further petition if you will vouchsafe it may not staye there neither, but that it may come to Her Majestie's sight, which truly will be most

* So Thomas always calls the Protestant bishops.

for the honor of your cause, at least soe far forthe for this affair yourselfe, that if you or any other should stande uppon any points of policy to the contrarie, more than we stand upon our own lives in trial of God's truth, yet there are thousands, as it may be presumed, even of your side which rather put it vp to Her Majestie with as common a crie to have it granted, rather, I say, than this triall, soe much importing them, should not be seene. A matter now, therefore, of some weight it is, whereof the credit either of your, or of oure side, doth lie in bleedinge, as it were. And if your confidence in your cause for the truth to be on your side, be anything at all, it behoveth that your having gone soe farr to labour as much as we, by like petition that the matter may come to open trial, and the learned of both sides to have open audiences; which God of His mercie grant, to Whom we commend you, wishinge you noe worse than to ourselves.

"Dated vppon the day of the Exaltation of the Holie Crosse of Christe the xiv. day of September, 1580.

"T. P., in Domino."

We now proceed to give a copy of Pounde's famous six reasons, of which, as we have seen in the first part, he gave a copy to his adversaries Tripp and Crowley; these will be followed by his correspondence with Tripp, and his letter to Sir

Christopher Hatton. All these form part of the same collection in Vol. cxlii., State Papers, *Domestic, Eliz.*, No. 20.

"The viith of September, 1580.

"Sixe reasons sett downe to shewe that it is noe orderly way in controversies of faithe to appeal to be tryed only by Scripture (as the absurde opinion of all the Sectaries is), but to the sentence and definition of the Catholike Churche by whome as by the Spouse of Christe, always inspired with the Holy Ghoste, the Holy Scripture is to be judged.

"*Fyrste*, consider well these wordes of our Savioure in sendinge vs to the Scriptures, saying, 'Searche the Scriptures for you thinke to have eternall life in them, and those are they that beare witnesse of Me.' Marke well these wordes, I pray, that the Scripture is but witnesse-bearer to the truthe; and not the judge to discerne of truth, for judgment given belongeth not to the witnesse-bearer, althoughe he be as a rule to leade, and directe the judge in true judgment. But what if this witnesse shoulde qe corrupted, as no man will deny but it may, yet this judge to whome the Holy Ghoste is promised, will finde it and reforme it : as shortly we will see by a true English Bible which is cominge forthe. Understand, therefore, my reasons why of necessitie the Churche must be judge of the Scripture, and take your pen, and confute them, I say to you, if you can. The first is because the written texte is mute and dumb, utteringe nothinge to us from the booke, but onely the wordes, and not the sense, wherein the life, as it were, of the Scripture consistethe, and what definitive sentence can suche a judge give to over-rule the conceited minde of an opiniative man, whiche hathe noe evident meanes to pronounce any judgment against him, but onely to showe him a dumb sign in writinge, which a wrangler may construe still to his own vnderstandinge against all the worlde.

"*The seconde* is because the Holy Scripture, as St. Augustine saithe, is very full of harde and deepe mysteries; insomuche that when Honoratus saide to him (as many unlearned men say nowe-a-days), that he understoode it well enoughe without helpe of any instruction, 'Say you,' saith he, 'you wold not take upon you to vnderstande such a poet as Terence is, well without a master; and dare you rushe into the Holie Scriptures, whiche are soe full of divine mysteries, without a judge? All heare-sayes, saith he, come of nothinge else: *Nisi dum Scripturæ bonæ intelliguntur non bene*—'But while the good Scriptures are not well vnderstoode.' Hereto alsoe St. Peter, in his Seconde Epistle, ch. iii., beareth witnesse sainge, that many misunderstood St. Paule in many harde places perversely, to their owne perdition. But then you will saye the harde places may easily be vnderstoode by conference of the other Scriptures: we'll admit a childish reason for a worde or two; that because that might soe be amonge the humble-minded, therefore they must needes be soe, though men be never so perverse; yet give me leave to pushe you the one question farther to the quicke: how is it possible to know by any conference of the Scriptures, which is canonical Scripture, and which is not? Certainely if any infidell wolde denye the Olde Testament (as some hereticks in time past have done), and I pray God there be not many Atheistes at this day in Englande, which be farther gone than they; yea, if such an one sholde deny all the New Testament also, we have sure anchor-holde against him by the revelation of God, by His tradition to His Churche, which is the pillor and sure stay of truthe; which St. Augustine well seeinge, thought he might be bolde to say with due reverence to God and Holy Scripture bothe: 'I sholde not believe the Gospell except the authoritie of the Churche did move me thereto;' meaning that tradition of the universall Churche, and the testimonye of all the people of God, in whom the Holy Ghoste dwelleth, must justly move us to credit that whiche theire authoritie doth commande us to give creditt vnto. Therefore, let any man beware of flying from the Churche's judgment [of] the Scripture only; least the Scripture itself shoulde be vtterlie denied, as by some Atheistes in Englande (as I hearsay) it is already; and then might such infidells laughe all heretickes to scorne for robbinge themselves of theire defence. But now to returne to my purpose. If conference of one Scripture with another, might give light enough to all men, how happeneth it, that all sectes vsinge that conference, yet they can never agree in theire opinions, but divers men, and all, vsinge suche conference doe yet construe it diversly, the vttermoste shift they have is this, such a weake one as it is, that the reader must give himselfe to prayer for the truth to be revealed vnto him; wherein, mark (I pray you) the intollerable pride of arrogant hippocrites, that they will first mistrust God's revelation of the truthe to His vniversall Churche, for the which Christ Himselfe hath prayed, and promised to teache them all truthe, and then most presumptuously to come, and tempt God to have that truthe onely revealed to themselves, which beinge revealed, many hundreth years agone, and defined in Generall Councells by all the holie Fathers, where the Holy Ghoste is alwaye present, or at least by the holie Doctors in their writinges set downe, yet they will not believe, nor harken vnto it. Yet this is their course, and soe, as they say, forsothe, they doe all pray very hartilie, thoughe few of them can wringe out any teares in theire prayers, but yet with suche a faithe in the Lorde (as theire owne tearme is) that they doe all verilie believe the truthe is revealed vnto them, and yet, forsooth, they must needes be all deceived, as longe as they dwell in dissention, and are not in errors only, but one contrary to another; who now must be the judge to trie the spirits whether they be of God or noe, but only the Churche, or else shall they not be tried at all, but continuall permission for infinite legions of lyinge spirits to be still undetected, that they may seduce more and more.

"*The third* reason is, because St. Peter saieth plainly that no Scripture is to be taken after any private interpretation. For it was not uttered after the will and phantasie of man, but as holie men of God spake it, inspired by the Holie Ghost. Yet most contrary to this expresse rule, every private man shall have libertie to enterpret it to his own perverse will, after a private enterpretation, otherwise than at first it was inspired to the holie men, if every man may appeale from the ecclesiasticall sense of the universall Churche to the text itselfe, as he understandeth it.

"*The fourth* reason is, because by appealinge onely to the Scriptures, you seeme to give men libertie to deny all vnwritten verities, which we have received of the Churche, either by expresse definition in Generall Councell, or else by tradition. And I believe at my first naminge of vnwritten verities, Mr. Crowley and his fellows will laugh streight way, as though suche were but fables; but to temper their follie, I will not say their pride, a little in that point, I aske them all this question: how they prove the Trinitie of Persons, and Vnitie of Substance, by expresse Scripture, or the two distinct natures in Christe, and but one Person, or God the Father to be *ingenitus;* or the proceedinge of the Holie Ghoste, bothe from the Father, and the Sonne, as from one Fountaine? Or the descendinge of Christ downe into hell, plain worde of Scripture beinge therefore of many now-a-daies flatly denied? Or the custome of baptizinge of infantes, seinge the Scripture saith rather as though they sholde be taught first theire faith before they were baptized; sayinge, 'Goe and teache all nations baptizinge them in the name,' &c.? Or why we sholde keepe the Sunday now at all, and not Saturday rather, which was the Jewes' Saboth day, that the Scripture speaketh of to be sanctified, although youre Puritans which goe to ploughe upon the Church's holidayes, seem not yet to know the Sundaye for any of theire making; or why we sholde not abstaine now still like the Jewes from strangled meates, as the Apostles once decreed in the Acts, and by noe express Scripture againe abrogated; yea, then, why may not any hereticke deny all three Creedes, both the Apostles' Creede, the Nicene Creede, as it is called, and the Creede of Athanasius, seeinge never a one of those is written in Scripture expressly, but all lefte us by tradition onely, upon credit of the Churche. Mark you not how these Bedlam Scripture-men wolde shake all the foundations of our Christian faith, by bindinge us to believe nothinge but Scripture. Do not these blind guides, think you, leade a trim daunce towards infidelitie? Thus much of the fourth reason.

"*The fifth* is, because without a certain judge for interpretation of Scripture, this absurdity wolde follow, that God, which is the Author of all perfection, and disposeth everything in stricte and decent order, had left His universall Churche on earthe in this confusion, that whensoever any doubtfull question sholde arise vpon construction of His holie will, there were no provision at all ordayned by God, for deciding of all suche strifes, and preservation of concorde amonge His people. And then certainely the Kingdome of God's Churche were not so well provided for in their government, as every civil kingdome is by policy of carnall men, amongst whome none almost are soe barbarous, but that they have counsellors for guidance of their estate, and judges for expoundinge, and executing of their lawes; as well as lawes written, or else it were rediculous. Wolde not he be counted a very wise man, thinke you, in one of our parliaments, which wolde step upp like a greate bragger, and persuade all his fellowes that for as much as they had a noble and ancient law left written vnto them, the realme sholde have no longer neede from henceforth of any prince, nor any rulers, nor peers, nor judges, nor justices, nor civil magistrates, but every man uppon his worde, for the warrant, wolde be content to govern himselfe orderlie by the lawe written, which as his wisdom thincks is plaine enoughe? And trulie ridiculous be they, but muche more to be laughed at, which will have the Scripture the onlie judge for every man to appeale vnto, and refuse all authoritie of the Churche in expoundinge thereof. Now who knoweth not that the Arian heretickes produce forty places of Scripture for theire horrible heresie, more than the Catholics had against them, but all falsely vnderstoode, which, when it is soe misvnderstoode, and misapplied, then St. Augustine called it the heretickes' bow wherewith they shoote their owne venemous arrows. And Vincentius Lyrins saith it is then the sheep's clothing which the wolfe doth shrowd himselfe in, because that when a simple body feeleth the softnes, as it were, of his fleece, he sholde not mistrust the tyranny of his teethe; that is to say, of his false constructions of Scripture, wherein he wolde devour his soule; so did the devill himselfe alledge Scripture unto Christ, and as oft as any hereticks alledge Scripture to us against the Catholic faithe, so oft, sayth Vincentius, we may be out of doubt the devyell dothe speake vnto us by theire mouthes, and sayth vnto us, even as he did vnto *Christ, *Si filius Dei es mitte te deorsum;* as much as to say—If thou wilt be the Son of God, and professor of His holie Gospell, cast thyselfe downe from the highe authoritie, and traditions of this Catholike Churche; whome, if we ask again, why we sholde do this, saythe Vincentius, they come out with *Scriptum est*, etc., because it is written, search in the holie book, and from thence thou mayst learne a new lesson of Me how to be a right Christian; to whom we must saye, *Vade Sathan non tentavi*, and that with great fervour of faythe; for more perilous is the temptation of such a flattering serpent, sayth St. Augustin, than the roaring of an angry lyon, because the one we flie from with feare, but the other with enticing may come the nearer to stinge us.

"*The sixth reason*, most weighty of all is this; because if you will refuse the authoritie of the Churche's absolute judgement upon the Scripture's true sense, you shall soone come plainly to denie the Holie Ghost to be the Spirite of Truth, which uppon the Apostles, and all the faithfull, was sent downe with visible signs, and with His Churche it is promised to remaine vnto the worlde's ende, by the wordes of our Saviour, 'I will ask My Father, and He shall sende you another comforter to tarry with you for ever, the Spirit of Truthe;' and a little after thus—'The Holie Ghoste the comforter Whome My Father will sende in My name shall teach you all truth.' So the Churche is the surest judge, and none surer but the Churche for all men in doubts of Scripture, because it hathe a promise that it shall never err in judgment, which is notably confirmed by the Prophet Esay, sayinge, 'This is My covenant with them, saith the Lord, My Spirit which is in thee, and My worde which I have put in thy mouthe, shall not departe out of thy mouthe, nor out of the mouthes of thy seed, nor out of thy seede's seede, nowe nor ever to the worlde's ende.' O most comfortable promise that the Spirit of Truth shall never departe out of ye Churche's mouth! O fit judge appointed to be judge of

Scripture, for our prophetes! Without presumption, remember then, I say to you, what a sottish opinion this is which is held to the contrary, that every private man, whom belike you will imagine to be one of the Church, shall have good leave to be his owne judge in vnderstandinge of Scripture, as your crafty men are, and yet that the authorities of the whole vniversall Churche shall not presume to take any judgment vpon them. Granting this, as you must needes, that the Churche, which is our Mother, as the Scripture saithe, must needes teach vs all her children, at first to believe in God, sayinge faithe must come by hearinge, and also to know the Scriptures; and yet that the same Churche beinge the pillar, and sure staye of truthe, shall not be absolute judge, and imperiall schoolmistress, to teache vs all how to believe in God, and how to vnderstande the Scriptures. For this blindness of your hearts, I may say as justly to you, as St. Paule saide to the Galatians, *O insensati*, etc.— O you foolish fellows, who hathe bewitched you not to obey vnto the truth? which even of infants and suckling babes (as it were) is discerned as cleare as the sun. Soe that you must not disdaine Mr. Tripp, to be tripped in this matter for a silly seducer, to maintaine as you doe, all so gross an opinion, beinge the forest indeede for all such foxes to litter their whelps in. Therefore, to conclude this assertion, acquite yourselves, as well as you can, why you may not all be justly subjected to deny the descending of the Holie Ghoste vnto the Church, for as much as you refuse the Churche's sentence in judgement, with whome the Holie Ghoste is promised alwayes to remaine, and in truthe to direct them.

"*Hæc est fides mea quia est Catholica*—'This is my faith because it is ye Catholic faithe.'

"THOMAS POUNDES." *

Mr. Thomas Pounde to Mr. Tripp.

"To Mr. Tripp the viij. of September.

"For as much at my requeste to you yesterday, and to Mr. Crowley, if ye be worthyie the naminge, makinge it, as I did, vpon my knees, not to you, as I tolde you, but for you to witnesse, and present to Her Majestie, and to all the Councell, as the common petition of God's afflicted in Englande, for the Catholike faithe, that it might please them to admit the learned indeede of our side, with the best learned of yours, to open audience, either by disputation, or by sermons enterchangeably hearde accordinge to the lawes and conditions of an orderly

---

* Mr. Dodd, *Church Hist.*, vol. ii., p. 153, briefly notices Pounde. "A gentleman of considerable fortune. He was a great supporter of Missioners, and suffered much for his religion in prison in Queen Elizabeth's reign. He was a man of letters, and published a small treatise entitled *Six Reasons*, &c. This was answered by a work called '*An Answer to Thomas Pounde's Six Reasons, wherein he sheweth that the Scripture must be judged by the Church.* By Robert Crowley. London. 4to, 1581.'"

conference, indeed as the weight of the cause doth require hereupon, for that I say you pretended to like well of it for youre parte, and promised all oure companie making the like meanes vnto you, for to preserve, and further oure saide petition; therefore I have here set downe our supplication to theire honors, so that as you see in all the Catholicks' names vniversally, to save you some labour in movinge of it with as manie of vs as here that may be spoken with, we hartilie pray you to preferre, and put upp to ye Councell accordinge to youre promise. Signifeynge thus vnto you besides, to certifie that, if free license may be granted for the choice of all oure side, either within or without the realme of Enlande, to come to this conference with good and safe conduct vpon the honoure of the Queene's Majestie's edict published in print, or if that be thought too muche, yet at the least for the choice of all oure side within the realme, as reason is, whencesoever they are to be removed uppon offeringe themselves voluntarily for this purpose, otherwise we are not so simple as to thinke ourselves satisfied with youre offering to call out vs the inferiors here now left abowte London in prison, if you should meane it to suche a conference, nor yet soe presumptuous as to take upon us to be the men meete to enter into suche a matche. Soe muche of the common cause. Now, touchinge my defence against you all, which I delivered you yesterday in writing, to feel your confidence in youre cause, beinge suche a question as knitts up all the contentions between us in one knot, and the absurdity which you helde, as I knew you wolde, beinge youre strongest castle. For as much now as the Bishop of London's warrant was made out for me, sen'night agone, to be removed very shortly to Storforde Castell, all alone there to be kept close prisoner, and havinge no great hope of any stay thereof, but rather of the lesse favor for this plainness in truth, whiche is wont, as you know, to breed noe friends; therefore I require you to answer my defence sincerely, soe as the reputation of youre best learned may lye upon it, at the last issue, without pleadinge vnprivitie to youre penman's handling of the matter. Settinge all myne entirely together, being but a sheete of paper, which doinge, as before I require you, while I may, before we be muzzled upp, then afterwardes in God's name bringe it to the hammer, and turne it, and wend it as you list; but yet save the poore man's neck whole if it lye in you, for at Mr. Crowley's watch-worde, that the sworde was nearer our necks than we thought for, of all syllogisms, a slidinge knot you knowe is the crookedest to be answered. We may be so weary of this pininge in prison so many years, without seinge the whole conversion of our country, which we ought to thirst for, that we are enforced to be plainer with you than they that are abroade at libertie, and not so tainted up in stinckinge prisons, as most of us already are, and all of us shortly may looke to be. Moreover, touchinge my trippinge of you somewhat sharply in the latter end of my defence, verily you might impute it but truly to your own provoking us all, by suche blaspheminge as youre fellow used the day before, so loude as all men might heare, bothe against the holie Masse, and against blessed St. Francis, whom your fellow burthened untruly with wickedness not to be named, he beinge one of the miracles of the worlde for perfit holinesse, as well in himselfe as in his posteritie, althoughe among soe much corn, there may be some cockell founde, as well as there was one weede among our Saviour's twelve holie flowers. Neverthelesse, to make you part of amends, I humble myselfe to you this good day vpon my knees, if that will assuage you for it, beseechinge you for Christ's sake, to dwell noe longer in heresie, to be worthie to be called foxes, as in the canticle youre name is, for vndermininge of God's vine yard. But yield to the truthe in time, whiche either you must all yelde to at last, or else it will crushe you all to pieces, for the citie of God is built upon soe highe a hill, and a rock soe invincible, that the weakest soldier, which is in it, may throwe out a stone to hit down any Golias amonge you to the grounde. Sigh over youre citie, therefore, if you be wise, and cease youre batteringe in vaine against the wall upon the rock, for as one sayth truely, against this wall whosoever setteth his force, doth but batter himselfe to pieces; when hell gates shall not prevaile against it, what can the force of a few fleshly men prevaile against it. God illumine you, and bless you, even as I would wishe to mine owne soule. The viij. of September.

"Your well wisher,

"T. P."

Mr. Tripp's answer.

"Mr. Pounde, touchinge youre letter meant privately, wherein yow require my answer to youre Six Reasons, cravinge some pardon for youre pleasant allusion to my name, that is not anythinge to me, for either I can be contented to let it pass, or answere it with the like, if I might be bolde to tell you that all youre Six Reasons weigh not one Pounde, as shall appeare by that which shall be answered. I was not minded, to tell you the truthe, to have answered them at all, Mr. Crowley vndertakinge to answer them, and he havinge your copie, of whose sufficiency in answering I doubt not; and if you meane to continue interchange of replie, and answere enoughe to encownter with one, hande to hande. It is sayde, *Ne Hercules quidem contra duos.* I confess myselfe the weaker of the two, and therefore thought to have abstayned. But I will yield my answere to you at my leasure; howbeit, I think yow will not thinke it meete that the credit of the best learned on oure side sholde depende upon my answere, noe more than the creditt of your whole cause, and of the best learned on youre side on your defence. For it were noe reason that youre learned men sholde be discredited wholie by youre slender handlinge of the cause, or that youre cause sholde wholie quaile by youre defence, or ours by mine, except both you and I could bringe all that the best learned of bothe parties are able to bringe. Howbeit, if your reasons be overweighed, I wishe you sholde in sinceritie yelde, rather to save your creditt to confesse an error in yeldinge to the thruthe. But for this matter the event shall show where truth moste resteth.

"Touchinge your supplication to the Queen in Councell, I am ready to preferr the same, but this I think to be a defect in it, that preferringe it in the name of all, and avouchinge it to be done with consent of a few, yow only subscribe your name. I suppose it were meete that a few more sholde subscribe with you, lest you may seem to have done it of youre owne head onely. Bethinke you whether I advise you well or not, and soe returne it to me againe. Fare you well, this xiith of September, 1580.

"Youres in the Lord, wishinge to yow as to myselfe.
"HENRIE TRIPP."

"To Mr. Tripp again the xivth of September.

"Sir,—I thanke you for undertakinge to answere me at length, though at your leasure, as partely indeed you pleaded some want of leasure for any suche matters, at my first deliveringe of it. Againe, some indifference you seem to shewe, that you would not have me overcharged with twaine at once; but youre cominge in cowples at first to conferre with every single man alone in theire chambers, was not soe even as youre pretence. Moreover, you have robbed yourselfe of halfe the glorie of your victorie in accomptinge my reasons to be soe light and soe easy to be overweighed, and yet that they sholde be so longe in counterpassinge. If they had been anythinge weighty they might have asked some tyme to chew vpon them, but beinge of noe weight you might have stamped, and stormed by this time, in a meat morter, soe as they sholde never have stuck in any bodies teeth, as otherwise perchance they will, without they be well and soundly answered, indeede better then in playing with my name, which in truth, I cannot deny, you beinge without malice, as by likelihoode of your pleasant vein, which I can well enough beare, I hope it will end well; I urge you to no haste in weighing them, lest you sholde mistake youre weights, and weigh either by weights, or in ballance not scaled, nor allowed by the clerks of the market, throughout the Catholick Christian comon weale. In which behalfe I warne you before hand, in the wordes of the Holie Ghost Whose cause it is, saying, *Statera justa, et æqua sint pondera*— 'Let balance be true and weights upright.' And then, I say, 'God speede the right.'

"Touchinge youre sendinge back of our supplication for a defect in it, as you pretende, in havinge noe more men's handes to it but mine alone, truly you can witness sufficiently for me to the Councell, if I sholde neede to appeal therefore unto you, that it was the common requeste of the moste parte hereunto, your as well as myne, that you wolde make it to be preferred to the Councell, as theire common suit. Soe farr off I am, as you can witness for me, from movinge it onely of my owne head, which notice, therefore, of yours I rest upon as sufficient, I hope to answer for me. So much I presume you see, of your uprightness, for your profession sake, which partly I am enforced to, because I cannot well get the handes of close prisoners to it without risk of rebuke, both to themselves and their keepers. And besides that our keeper, I perceive, doth not well like the proceedinge it, as I suppose few doe of the deepest heads of your side, whatsoever some may persuade it. You will give me leave to be plaine with you, which cannot speake in these matters, but as I think. Moreover, if you woulde needes have any more handes to it, I wolde rather make humble suite that I might have leave to goe unto the handes of the chief, and best learned in England of our side, than present up the names in it of any persons more inferiour, whose petitions perchance wold be more contemned for their obstinancie, than by the tendering of it thus in all our names universally, by sufficient conjecture, as you see, that all other sorte are of the like minde that you here have found us. Let my offer, therefore, be sufficient for the matter, as I hope it may, seinge more than my life I cannot gage, otherwise if you require any more for your preferringe it, we may all well think that it is for some delay, or for some further ende, which I will drawe no man vnto. Howsoever, I offer myselfe vnto God's protection in so common a cause. At your choice, therefore, be it, whether you will prefer it accordinge to your promise, or else to abyde the danger of the discredite it may be to your side, as thoughe you were afraide to have it goe forward. Neverthelesse, I have added thus much more to it as a letter comes to, which I have written to the Lord of London, in the same behalfe, which I beseeche you cary to him, and our supplication again vnder seale also, to rest as muche longer at his deliberation what to doe in it, which if it come back any more, I thincke none of oure side neede to doubt what bad likinge of it you have to proceede.

"Almighty God blesse you, to Whome I commit you. 1580. Your well wisher in our Lorde.

"T. P."

"To the Righte Hon. Sir Christr. Hatton, Kt., Vice Chamberlaine to Her M[tie]·, and one of Her P. Councell.

"Your noble courtesie towards me, already shewed in writing so exceeding friendlie to my L., as you did of late, for some favor at lest towardes me for your sake, altho' it were but for a few days respite, to have some of my debts cleared before my removing, which yet wolde not be granted, terminge me, as you vouchsafed, your old acquaintance and companion, both in Courte, and before in Inns of Courte, dothe embolden me ofte times to beseech your honour, that you will not be denyed the obtaininge of so much favor towardes me, as that my man, or boy, may be admitted to me in this miserable and desolate place, to bringe my diet, or for any other servile service for necessitie of nature, although he sholde be searched, if any suche jelousie were of me, at all tymes of his repair. O God! Sir Christopher, I woulde you saw the spectacle of it, what a place I am brought into here! It is nothing but a large, vast room, cold water, bare walls, noe windows, but loupholes too high to looke out at, nor bed, nor bedsteade, nor place very fit for any, but the homliest thinge in the middest of the house, a highe pair of stockes, such a pair of urginalls,* as made my poor boy to see, although far too bigg either for his fingering, or footinge, all athwart my cold harbor, and nothinge else but chains enough, which yet I am not worthie of. And if there were neither meet, nor drink, neither for love nor money, then the end wolde be but short. 'And yet what is all this, or ten times more for Heaven, which upon this cause dependeth. Shall hunger, or cold, or

---

* *Urginals*, probably thumb-screws, from *Urgeo* to press.

stenchinge, or taintinge, or any kind of persecution, separate vs from the holie unitie of Christ's Church, for which He hath shedd His pretious Bloode? No, God defend, at youre mercie, and Her Majestie's I am, while our pining time continueth, whether this much respite, as I humbly sue for on my knees, shall be had or no, well hopinge if your honour will vouchsafe to present my petition, that her highness will not be soe vanquished by her vassals, but that even for her poeticall present's sake, which Her Majesty disdayned not to take at poore Mercurie's hands, if you remember it, at Killiegeworth Castle,* she will now vouchsafe, of her princely good nature, to give me as good a gifte again for double requitall thereof, as this suit comes to, especiallye knowinge as Her Highness well doth, what is written—That it is a blesseder thing to give than to take, wherein I humbly beseech your honor at your wisdom and discretion, to trie once more what stead you can stande me in, accordinge to youre goodwill, whereby for ever you shall bind me more and more unto. At Stortford, before my entering, ye 18th of September, 1580.

"Youre servant to God in dayly prayer.

"THOMAS POUNDES."

* By this allusion to Kenilworth Castle, we may presume that Pounde had also acted there during the Queen's stay at that place. He had also, perhaps, presented the Queen, as he had done at Winchester College, with a poetical complimentary address.

Our confessor's zeal in challenging the ministers, and petitioning the bishop and Council, had the effect of convincing the Queen's Ministers that a conspiracy was on foot. Pounde soon felt the consequence (as we have already seen in the first part of this notice); the Bishop of London, Elmer or Aylmer, having removed him from his companions in the Marshalsea (September 18th, 1580), and sent him heavily ironed into solitary confinement at the then half-ruined episcopal castle of Bishops-Stortford. Pounde, therefore, on the eve of his departure, either delivered Father Campion's paper to the keeping of some one even less retentive of a secret than himself, or else communicated it through an unwillingness to be checkmated by the Bishop of London, whose conduct he regarded as a mere device to stop all mention of a public discussion, or from a conviction that Father Campion's challenge was much more calculated to embarrass the Council than his own had proved to be. Actuated by one of these motives, Pounde communicated the paper to his neighbour, Benjamin Tichborne, Tichborne to William Horde, and he to several others, and especially to Elizabeth Saunders, a Nun, sister to Dr. Saunders, who was at this time with the Italian expedition in Ireland.*

The paper or declaration of Father Campion was not printed, but circulated extensively in MS. It was called "The great bragge and challenge"—"A

* Simpson's *Campion*, p. 163.

seditious pamphlet," &c., and was regarded as a gauntlet thrown down by the Jesuits.* As the subject of our notice may (as before observed) be regarded as the author or first mover of this famous though simple declaration of intentions to the Council, we will make a short digression to mention a few instances of its effects.

John Watson, the pseudo-Bishop of Winchester, on the 18th of November, or thereabouts, laid hands on the above-named parties (except Tichborne), including the Nun, Elizabeth Saunders, and committed their bodies to the house of correction. It was about the same time that the copy with the letters, &c., of Thomas Pounde, were discovered, and sent by the Sheriff of Wilts to the Privy Council. From this time it became well known all over England, and many persons got into trouble for circulating copies of it.† Frequent mention is made of it amongst the State Papers. The following is a copy of the letter of the said Bishop of Winchester, and others endorsed, "18th of November, 1580. From the Bishop of Winchester and others, with the examination and other things taken of Dr. Saunders' sister apprehended at Alton and committed at Winchester.

---

* Mr. Simpson, in his very valuable Appendix of Father Campion's works, and of the numerous publications connected with him, mentions eight upon the subject of the challenge mentioned above.

† Simpson's *Campion*, p. 163, *Dom. Eliz.*, Ireland, State Paper Office, 17th February, 1581.

Also the confession of William Hoord touchinge the challendge of the Jesuites, whome they have committed likewyse at Winchester."*

"Our duties to your Hon. Lordshipps humblie remembered. For that of late in Hampsheer, there happened to be apprehended by Sir Richard Norton, Knt., one Elizabeth Saunders, the sister of Dr. Saunders, and a professed Nunn beyond the seas, as she saith, with whome were certain lewd and forbydden bookes, and the copye of a supplication, protestation, or chalendge, the which copye, together with her examinations, we have thought herewith to sende vnto youre honors. And for that we finde by her sayde examination grete dissimulation and varietie in her, and also grete obstinacie in her perseverance of her profession; we have thought thereupon presentlie to committ her to safe keping in the house of correction, within the Castle of Winchester, where she is to remain vntil such further order shall be taken for her, as by youre Lordshipps shall be thought mete. We have further thought good herewith, also, to send vnto your honours, the examination of one William Hoorde, gentleman, remaining at this present in the house of correction thither committed, for that he is a verie backwarde and obstinat person in matters of religion, and soe he continued all the tyme of Her Majestie's raigne,

* 1580. *Dom. Eliz.*, State Papers, Vol. cxliv., No. 3.

whome we believe to be the first bringer, and dispenser of the seditious challendge aforesaid in this countie; and yet beinge examined, refused to declare of whom he received the same. The rather we have signified the premises to your Hon. for that the sayd challendge at the first publication whereof, in these partes, seemed vuto such like backwarde persons, verie plausible. And soe we humblie committ your Honors to the tuicion of Allmightie God.

"St. Crosse, 18th November, 1580."

In *Dom. Eliz.*, Vol. cxlvii., Nos. 73, 74, 76 are other interesting papers upon the same subject. No. 74, which embodies the rest, is endorsed by Walsingham—"The declaration of Benjamin Tichbowrne's behaviour in bearing owt of one William Pittes, a scatterer of Campion's challenge, and a deliverer of lewd speeches touchinge Her Majestye and the present state. Also of the ill usage of one Edwardes by the sayd Tichbowrne's servant, for which the peace was graunted against Tichbowrne and his man. And lastly, how Mr. Tichbowrne, to encounter all the honest gentlemen in religion in the countie of Southampton, hath procured himselfe to be put in the commission of the peace there, by the meanes of the Lord Chief Baron, who countenanceth the sayd Tichbowrne."

This Mr. Pitts was charged (amongst other things) with giving out "That learned, and godlye persons who offered disputations, were refused to bee heard, saying it was odious that men's soules sholde hang in daunger by reason the sayd learned men were denyed audience. That he thought Her Majestye erred from the true fayth, saying that his daylie prayer was to bryng her to the Catholique faythe. *Item.* That hee asked one Lichepoole whether hee had not seen a coppie of a challenge made by one Campion, and other Jesuitts. Wherevnto Lichepoole answered that hee had seene no suche wryting. The sayde Pytts immediately pulled owte of his purse the coppie of the sayde challenge, and read it vnto the sayde Lichpoole, promising him a coppie of the same, if hee sente for it vnto his lodgings, and Lichpoole sending for the same, hee delivered the messenger the coppye thereof. When Sir John Fettiplace heard the confession of Lichpoole, and had reade the coppye of the challenge, he sent immediately to the lodgings of the sayd Pytts, to apprehend him, but the sayd Pitts was fledd."

Sir John then caused the house of Henry Pytts, the father of William, to be searched, but in vain, for William. "Neverthelesse, finding there a sister of Dr. Saunders, who is a professed Nun, and divers unlawfull bookes, with a challice, she was brought to the lord bishoppe, which Nun remayneth as yet in prison at Winchester."

The tale of Mr. Benjamin Tichborne is amusing. William Pitts was caught at Bath; from thence he wrote to Mr. Tichborne asking him to send the

Mayor of Bath a certificate, "under his hande and seale of armes," in his favour on divers points. Mr. Tichborne sent this letter, and one from himself, to Mr. Henry Pitts, the father, at Alton, for information and instructions in making the certificate. The messenger being a stranger, asked for Pitt's house, saying he had a letter for him from his son. One Edwards hearing this, got hold of the letter, and took it at once to the constable, who being from home, Edwards took it to one Mr. Stone, a lawyer, "by whose advice the letter was broken vpp to see the contents thereof." Mr. Tichborne being indignant at their impudence, sent his servant to Stone's house, who luckily for himself, was from home. He then proceeded to Edwardes' house, and calling him out, gave him a very severe beating, and said he would have used Stone much worse, if he could have found him, "for breaking vpp of his master's letter."

William Pitts was sent from Bath to Winchester, and committed to gaol for trial at the approaching assizes, and Mr. B. Tichborne and his servant were bound over likewise to appear at the same assizes, for the assault. William Pitts, however, "on the 10th of February, 1581, broke the Queen's gaol and fled, having horses layd readie for him as it may appear."

Mr. Tichborne completely outwitted his adversaries by getting into great favour with the Lord Chief Baron, who on his way to Winchester assizes honoured him with a visit at Alton, and there made him a county magistrate. Mr. Tichborne told his lordship the whole case about the letter opening, and the assault by his servant, for which they were bound over to appear at the assizes. On making him a magistrate, the Chief Baron said to Mr. T., "Now you are fellow with those that bound you to the peace." At Alton also, the judge issued a warrant at Mr. Tichborne's request, against the unlucky lawyer, and Edwards, who appearing before him there, after reviling them, he bound them over in xl*l*. a piece, to appear before him at the assizes, saying, "I'll do nothing here unto you, but that which I shall doe, shall be done in the face of the whole shire, and Sir Richard Norton shall not out-countenance this matter." On Stone and Edwards appearing at the assizes, the judge stopped the lawyer in opening his cause against Mr. Tichborne and his servant, saying that he would not hear him, but told him that he was expelled the temple [struck off the rolls] " for his misbehaviour; that he was verye sawcie to open the sayd letters, and threatned that he should take good heede that hee came no more before him, affirminge that if hee did, hee sholde know the pryce thereof."

The judge passed over the escape of William Pitts "slightly ; saying also to the gaoler that hee should paye x*l*. for the same escape, and saying openly that the sayd gaoyler needed not to receave anye prisoner into the Queen's gaoyle, sent by the lord bisshoppe, or others, except it were for matter of the Crown only."*

The last instance we will notice is a letter dated 27th of June, 1586, from Walton, the keeper of the Fleet Prison, to Sir T. Walsingham, stating (*inter alia*), "Here is now remaining one Stephen Vallenger, committed from the Starre Chamber, by Her Majestie's Privy Counsell for publishing certain libels of Edmund Campion, and hath been committed these iiij. years." †

To return now to the object of our narrative. The Queen and her advisers having in vain tried by every means of promises and persuasion to induce Father Campion, who had now been apprehended, to apostatize, or betray his friends, now determined to use him severely. He was several times cruelly racked, the first time being either on Sunday the 30th of July, or the next day, the anniversary of our holy Father St. Ignatius' death. It was falsely given out by the preacher at Paul's Cross, and by the ministers of nearly all the churches in London, that Father Campion was yielding, and had confessed various

---

* Mr. Henry Pitts had married a sister of Dr. Saunders, and one of his sons was a fellow of the New College, Oxford, from whence he escaped to Rome. Mr. B. Tichborne was a great favourer of Papists, and was himself suspected, not having been to the "Lord's Supper" for some years past; and Mrs. T., and others of his house, refused to go to church. He gave warning to divers Catholics to fly from the diocese, who would otherwise have been apprehended by the brutal bishop. See State Papers, *Eliz.*, Vol. cxlvii., No. 76.

† *Dom. Eliz.*, State Papers, Vol. cxc., No. 55, 27th June, 1586.

matters, places, and persons. On the 4th of August the Council wrote to, amongst others, the keepers of Wisbeach Prison, whither Pounde had been removed by Aylmer the Bishop, from Bishops-Stortford, shortly before, "That whereas Campion had confessed that he delivered a copy of his challenge to one Norris a Priest, commonly remaining about London; that he delivered another to one Pounde, then prisoner in the Marshalsea, who is thought to have dispersed the same abroad; that one Stephens brought the said Pounde to speak with Campion at Throckmorton House in London, and further that Pounde directed Campion by a token to one Dimock to speak with the Earl of Southampton," the said keepers were to examine Pounde on the matter. On the 14th of August the Council wrote to Bishop Aylmer, ordering him to send his prisoner Thomas Pounde from Wisbeach to the Tower, where Lieutenant Hopton is to receive him into his custody to be jointly examined with Campion, upon matters confessed by Campion about him.

When Pounde saw the long list of interrogations drawn up, as they purported to be, from Father Campion's confessions, he was wounded to the heart. Could it be that the man whom he had taken for the greatest champion of Catholicism, had turned traitor? So the same zeal which before had led him to disperse Father Campion's challenge, now led the impulsive and sanguine Pounde to an act of imprudence equally grave in its consequence. He wrote a letter to Campion, urging him to behave like a man, telling him of the reports of his backsliding that were every where current, and asking him for authentic information of what he had done. This letter he gave to his keeper, who promised for a fee of four marks to have it privately delivered to Campion. The man took the money and kept it, but the letter he gave to Hopton, who opened, and read it, and closed it again, as if it had never been tampered with, and told the keeper to deliver it to Campion, and to bring back the reply. Father Campion wrote off a note to his friend, no authentic copy of which is preserved. The most likely record of it occurs in the reports of the trials of Lord Vaux and others in the Star Chamber, 15th November, 1581 (Harl. MSS., 859), and of Father Campion himself, where there was "a letter produced said to be intercepted, which Mr. Campion should seem to write to a fellow prisoner of his, namely, Mr. Pounde; wherein he did take notice that by frailty he had confessed of some houses where he had been, which now he repented him of, and desired Mr. Pounde to beg him pardon of the Catholics therein, saying that in this he rejoiced, that he had discovered no things of secret, nor would he, come rack, come rope." What the real meaning of this letter was can only be guessed at; Pounde's letter, to which it was a reply, was never produced, and the above sketch of it was probably a guess of Father Parsons. The natural meaning of Father Campion's words is that he discovered nothing that had not been already publicly known through the confessions of other men.* There is no record of the examination of Pounde in the Tower on this occasion, if indeed any took place. Perhaps none did; the Council may have feared to bring him into connection with Campion, whom they would never allow to be publicly interrogated about his reported confessions.

Pounde was present with Mr. Sherwin, Mr. Bosgrave, afterwards Father Bosgrave, and others of the Catholic prisoners in the Tower, at the famous public conference in the chapel of the Tower, appointed to be held on the last day of August, 1581, by the Bishop of London, in obedience to the Lords of the Privy Council, between Nowell, Dean of St. Paul's, and Day, Dean of Windsor, on the one side, and Father Campion on the other, which lasted for several days. During the conference, Dean Nowell complains of "Pounde's odious interpellations (as 'we know you to be a good Terence man'), and his most scornful looks through his fingers, staring at him (Nowell) continually whilst he was reasoning with Master Campion, to put him out of his memory;" whereupon Nowell broke out with "*os impudens.*"

Knowing Thomas' great zeal and courage, and calling to remembrance his spirited affair with Bishop

---

* Simpson's *Campion*, p. 247, seq., where the author at considerable length, and most lucidly, proves the reported confessions of the blessed martyr to have been base and wicked forgeries.

Horne of Winchester, we may well imagine how galled he must have been at the insolence of these two deans, and the unjust and cruel treatment of Father Campion, as recorded in the account of this long conference; of which the blessed martyr himself, in his reply complains—" As to the conditions of the discussion, though they were clearly most unjust, yet he accepted them; he had challenged them; they had met him on the field he had indicated; but they had taken care to deprive him of his arms; for the arms of the disputant are books and meditations: no notice had been given him of the conference; no time for thought; as for books, even his notes had been taken from him. Was it an answer to his challenge to rack him first, then to deprive him of all books, and to set him to dispute? When life was in question, with the gallows before, and the rack behind, the mind was hardly free for philosophy," &c.

Nowell's opening of the conference must have especially excited Pounde—"They had come to seek the truth; not for themselves, for they had found it, but to help Campion and his fellows, and to do them good, if God permitted."

If an impartial report had been given of the conference, it is more than probable that we should find many pungent "interpellations," &c., by Thomas, besides the above. Amongst the many converts of Thomas was our glorious martyr, Father Thomas Cottam, who suffered at Tyburn, May 30, 1582, in the thirty-third year of his age.* He entered the Society in Rome, April 8, 1579. He was a native of Lancashire, born of Protestant parents, and brought up as such. Having made his earlier studies at home, he came to London to complete them, and to seek his own fortune. Here it pleased God that he should be introduced to, and become on the most intimate terms of friendship with our noble Thomas Pounde, who was not then become a prisoner for the Faith. Father Cottam was not only a Protestant at that time, but his habits were not of the most praiseworthy kind. Thomas, however, by the cogency of his reasoning, and the example of his own holy life, not only converted him to the Catholic faith, but wrought a total reformation in him, changing him into another man; so much so that he resolved to give himself up entirely to God, and the service of His Church. He left England for the Seminary of Douay, carrying with him, and retaining as he always did to the last, a present and lively recollection of Pounde, the father of his soul, and of the everlasting debt of gratitude he owed to that holy man, through whom he had gained the precious treasure of faith.

In a letter to his benefactor, dated Ascension Day, 12th May, 1575, worthy of record, he says, "Your charity, like its author, is eternal; and as there is no comparison between things eternal, and perishable

* *Vide* Challoner's *Missionary Priests;* Father More's *Hist. Prov. Angl.;* Father Bartoli, *Inghil.;* and Father Tanner.

goods, between time and eternity, so am I neither able by word or writing to sufficiently express the testimony of my gratitude, I owe you. I remember when you were to me a consoler in my solitude, the guide of my path, my helper in my afflictions, and my refuge in need.

"Through you the Divine mercy recalled me from my wanderings; raised me up when fallen; sustained me in my wavering; preserved me in my trials; restored me when lost. So great a thing is it to possess a faithful friend; and such you have well shown yourself to me; and at the same time the vast difference there is between an honest and conscientious Christian, and an ordinary one, and one of pleasures.

"I had already begun to know vice (which I deeply lament). Now I follow virtue, and wonderfully it refreshes my soul, now freed from earthly cares, and safe from my enemies, and in no great fear of hell. These are great things indeed, and for all of which I am indebted to you; but that by far the greatest of all, which the Holy Ghost, by the mouth of the Apostle saith, *Testimonium reddit spiritui nostro, quod sumus filii Dei.**

"I beseech you by the same Holy Spirit; by Christ this day ascending into Heaven; by the Eternal Father at Whose right hand He sitteth; by the Omnipotent and Immortal God, Three in One, that you be always mindful of me, and sometimes

* Rom. viii. 16.

solace me by your letters. I will implore this same God, even to my latest breath, that He may long preserve you safe, with the highest increase of His honour and merits, and at last crown you with a holy end! Farewell!"*

We conclude this notice of our noble confessor of the Faith, and dear brother in Christ, with an expression of admiration at the providence of God displayed in regard to him, decreeing that (although he was almost an equal object of dread and hatred to the adversaries of the Faith as the blessed martyr Father Campion himself, yet, nevertheless) he should not be led forth to consummate his victory at Tyburn, as so many other of his contemporaries were—a consummation he had so long sighed after, daily expected, and was so well prepared for—but that he should be reserved for a far more painful, because tedious martyrdom of thirty years of incarceration, and chains, in loathsome dungeons.

* More, *Hist. Prov. Angliæ*, l. iv., n. vii., p. 127.

Book the Second.

GEORGE GILBERT, S.J.

GEORGE GILBERT, S.J.

In proportion to the exertions of the Fathers of the Society of Jesus and the Secular Clergy of England in defending the orthodox faith from the attacks of its bitter enemies, was the violence with which heresy assaulted all professors of that faith, and endeavoured to shake their constancy.

By a recent Act of Parliament (16th January, 1581)* it is enacted that every one from the age of sixteen years shall be fined twenty pounds sterling (or eighty gold crowns) per month, reckoning the year at thirteen months, who failed to attend the Protestant church: also, every one either going to a Priest for confession, or who should be reconciled to the Catholic Church, was declared guilty of high treason; for, indeed, they construed all this to be "a seducing of Her Majesty's subjects from their allegiance." The penalty for attending Mass was one hundred marks and imprisonment for one year, and until payment of the fine, in most cases amounting to imprisonment for life. A Priest, for saying Mass, was sentenced to the

* 23 Eliz., cap. i. See Madden, *Penal Laws*, p. 153.

same imprisonment, and fined in double that amount. An occurrence somewhat ludicrous, though very characteristic of our judges of that time, happened under this Act. A certain Secular Priest was accused of having received Holy Orders abroad, contrary to the statute, &c.; he was tried, and acquitted by the jury for want of sufficient proof of his ordination. After this verdict was pronounced, some obscure apostate came forward in court, and swore to having heard the Priest say Mass thirty years ago. Upon this the learned judge, without any fresh trial, actually condemned the *acquitted* party, because, said his lordship, he could not have said Mass if he had not been a Priest—*ergo*, &c.! As the unfortunate Priest was unable to pay such a fine, he was adjudged to what to him was tantamount to imprisonment for life.

"But to return," says Father More, from whom we are quoting, "to our more immediate matters. About this time, 1581, there was apprehended and cast into prison, under these laws, the Earl of Southampton, Lords Paget, Compton, Vaux, Sir Thomas Tresham, Sir William Catesby, Sir John Arundell, Sir Nicholas Poyntz, and Ralph Sheldon, Esq., Thomas Throckmorton, Esq., and many others, men of high family and wealth. And, amongst the rest of the most illustrious Catholics, the iniquitous knaves keenly hunted after George Gilbert, either because this noble youth far outstripped his companions in virtue, or else because they had discovered that he was almost always by the side of Father Parsons, as his faithful companion, guide, and supporter; and, had he fallen into their hands, he would inevitably have suffered the tortures of the Tower and the gallows of Tyburn." Thus Father More introduces to us the subject of of our narrative.*

This most excellent youth, George Gilbert, was a native of Suffolk. His father was a man of high rank and large property. For the first seventeen years of his life, which he spent in England, he was brought up in heresy, more by the fault of others than his own. He was professedly a Puritan; yet, though his faith was bad, his life was good. From his childhood his thoughts turned towards God and the things relating to his soul, and one of his most congenial occupations was to read spiritual books, and lay up for himself treasures of this kind. His was the praise and merit not to remain in error, but to set himself in the path of inquiry after the Catholic truth; which, having once embraced, so great was his delight in it, so holy his works, so upright his pursuit of its teachings, that after a novitiate of a few months, he was an example to, and the admiration of, veteran Catholics.

Before his conversion to the Catholic religion his chief delight was in the thought of arms and chivalry, which both suited his disposition, and for which his habit of body was in every regard admirably adapted. His graceful form, his pleasing countenance and

---

* More, *Hist. Prov. Angl.*, l. iii., n. 16, p. 82.

gentlemanly address, together with his high birth, made him a great favourite at the Court, which, both under Mary and Elizabeth, abounded more than ever with cavaliers, and was exceedingly gay.

For the sake of seeing, and being seen, he travelled to Paris, where he made so great a figure at Court in all "courtly" manners, and feats of chivalry, as to be there esteemed the "flower of the flock" among his compatriots. However, amidst all this, he preserved his soul intact; for, as is above observed, if his faith was unsound, his life was moral, deeming this to be of great importance, both out of a natural honesty, and a salutary regard to the public eye, which, as a foreigner, and in so large and criticizing a theatre as Paris, he both respected and feared; hence, he was jealous of his honour, and unwilling to appear to degenerate even in the eyes of strangers.

Father Thomas Darbyshire was at that time living in Paris, whose fame for virtue and learning was well known to Mr. Gilbert in England. His history forms the third part of this volume.

Mr. Gilbert began to treat with Father Darbyshire, at first upon terms of civility as a fellow-countryman, then on more intimate terms, and at last seriously upon religious subjects, which until then he had never done on account of the monstrous and impious doctrine of "Assurance of Salvation" professed by his sect of the Puritans. Being either moved with the eternal reasons propounded by Father Darbyshire, or else by the sanctity of life he noticed in him, doubts arose in his mind as to his real state, sufficiently strong to induce him at once to banish from his heart and mind all the follies of Calvin, and, at the same time, all love and desire of Court custom and deeds of arms. Travelling from Paris to Rome, he gave himself up to Father Parsons, who was at that time confessor or penitentiary in St. Peter's Church, for instruction in the Catholic religion. This ended in his speedy conversion and reconciliation to the Church; this was in 1579. Father Parsons stood his godfather at his confirmation. From that time, though the new convert still pursued his studies, and learned the accomplishments for which Italy was then famous—riding, fencing, vaulting, and the like, for he was of stalwart growth *—yet he secretly added all kinds of religious exercises, such as prayer, fasting, mortification, and liberal almsgiving. He wished to expend his first fervour in a pilgrimage to Jerusalem; but Father Parsons persuaded him rather to return to England, and lay out his money in assisting Priests, and on other means of advancing the Catholic cause.

Strengthened with admirable precepts, he returned to England altogether a different man than the gay George Gilbert who had left it a few years before. He was then in the flower of his youth; an only child and an orphan, with a rich inheritance in Suffolk and other counties at his free disposal, which he

---

* At the end of this Life will be found a quaint description of Mr. Gilbert (*Dom. Eliz.*, State Papers, P. R. O., Vol. cxl., No. 62).

liberally expended in relieving the needs of the Catholic poor. He contracted an intimate friendship with Thomas Pounde, Esq., of Belmont, who had been long buried in prison for the cause of the Faith. In his frequent visits to him in the gaol he sometimes remarked that many of the incarcerated Catholics suffered much in the winter from cold and bad clothing; these he would immediately, at his own expense, furnish with new and respectable clothes. Mr. Pounde recommended to his charity a large community of Nuns, who had been expelled from their convent in England, and had taken refuge in Flanders, and on that account were reduced to such poverty that amongst the great number there were only two Breviaries wherewith to say Divine Office; and, indeed, one of these was only a manuscript copy, and so old, torn, and worn out by constant use as to be almost unserviceable. The holy virgins did not ask relief in their other necessities, but in this only, in order to enable them to sing the praises of God, and for the consolation of their hearts. The reprinting would cost them three hundred scudi. George Gilbert sent them six hundred, asking only in return the favour of their making him a present of the old torn manuscript copy; and this because it had been used for many years by one of these Religious, who was then very aged, and held in great repute for sanctity.

One result of his return to England was that he drew together and organized divers principal young men, forming them into a club or association for promoting the cause of the Catholic religion; binding themselves to perform the two functions of preparing Protestants and conducting the Priests, and, besides, to procure alms for the common fund, out of which the Priests were supplied. Their promise entailed upon them great sacrifices; they determined to "imitate the lives of the Apostles, and devote themselves wholly to the salvation of souls and conversion of heretics." They promised to "content themselves with food and clothing, and the bare necessaries of their state, and to bestow all the rest for the good of the Catholic cause." The Association was solemnly blessed by Pope Gregory XIII., 14th April, 1580. They soon became known as "subseminaries," "conductors, companions, and comforters of Priests;" "lay-brothers," out of whom the Jesuits were accused of getting "either all or most part of their riches" before turning them into officers and solicitors; "inferior agents," "lay-assistants to straggle abroad and bring in the game," whose business it was not to argue, but to pry in corners to get men to entertain conference with the Priest, or inveigle youths to fly over sea to the Seminaries."*

The Association consisted of many youths of noble parts, whom the example and exhortations of George Gilbert had inflamed to join in his efforts. They were men of birth and property, without the incum-

---

* Simpson's *Campion*, p. 157, quoting Gee, the apostate, *Foot out of the Snare*, &c.

brance of wives or offices; and thus free to devote themselves to the cause, they entered on their dangerous and difficult path with extraordinary joy and alacrity—every man offering himself, his person, his ability, his friends, and whatsoever God had lent them besides. Mr. Gilbert was the first—he was, in fact, the founder and the soul of the Association; other members were, Henry Vaux (Father Campion's old pupil), and Vaux's brother-in-law, Brooks, Charles Arundell, Charles Basset (great-grandson of Sir Thomas More), Edward and Francis Throgmorton, William Brookesby, William and Richard Griffin, Arthur Cresswell, Edward Fitton, Stephen Brinkley, Jervase and Henry Pierrepoint, Nicholas Roscarock, Anthony Babbington, Chideock ·Tichbourne, Charles Tilney, Edward Abingdon, Thomas Salisbury, Jerome Bellamy, William Tresham, Thomas Fitzherbert, John Stoner, James Hall, Richard Stanihurst (another of Father Campion's pupils), Godfrey Fuljambe (who afterwards did very little credit to the Association), and many others whom Father Parsons will not name for fear of compromising them. Amongst them must have been at one time Lord Oxford, Lord Henry Howard, Mr. Southwell, Lord Paget, and Mr. Pounde. Divers of these, with Mr. Gilbert, took lodgings together, and sojourned in the chief pursuivant's house in Fetter or Chancery Lane. This pursuivant had great weight with Aylmer, Bishop of London; they had also another powerful protector at Fulham, where was the focus of their peril, in the person of the bishop's son-in-law, Dr. Adam Squire, who was in their pay. Through the connivance of these men they were able to receive Priests, and to have Mass celebrated daily in their house, till the arrival of the Jesuits, when the times grew much more exasperated.

The necessity of this Catholic Association has been detailed in the Life of Thomas Pounde, and therefore need not be here repeated.

Father Parsons, under the disguise of a discharged soldier from the Low Countries, safely passed the eagle-eyed searchers at the port of Dover, and prepared the way for Father Campion's following as a "merchant of jewels"—most appropriate disguises, their mission being truly a warfare, and their business a merchandise of the "pearl of great price." Father Parsons reached Gravesend at midnight, and got to London and found our Mr. Pounde in the Marshalsea Prison. Great was the astonishment and joy of that noble champion of Christ when Father Parsons stood before him; but that joy could only be of a short duration, for the Father must be away again as quickly as possible ere he was recognized by others. Mr. Pounde, therefore, sent with all haste to acquaint Mr. Gilbert, than whom none of all the many Catholics in London could be more trustworthy or more acceptable to Father Parsons. The Father dined with the numerous Catholic prisoners, and afterwards committed himself to the guidance of one of the guests, "Mr. Edward Brookesby, who led him to a Catholic house in the City, a kind of club, where he found other gentlemen and Priests, and notably Mr. Gilbert."*

It was truly by an act of Divine Providence, in Mr. Gilbert's regard, that Father Parsons arrived that identical day in London, and that it occurred to Mr. Pounde, his friend, to recommend the Father to his hospitality, for on the same day there was a meeting about the settlements to be made on his intended marriage with a young heiress, to whom his friends had advised him to make advances. This lady was in every respect his equal in rank and fortune.

The very sight of Father Parsons so entirely changed him, inspiring him with so great a repugnance of this intended marriage, and of all other earthly things, that breaking off all further treaty about the match, he determined instead to enter upon a far different kind of love, and, with Father Parsons' approbation, to consecrate himself to God by a vow of perpetual chastity. This the Father would not at first allow him to do, though at last he gave permission for the vow "till the Catholic religion should be publicly professed in England."

He thereupon entirely devoted himself to Father Parsons as the individual companion of his journeys, and to be made useful by him for the good of the Catholic cause, even to the expending thereon his sweat and blood. He would not be admitted on

* This was no doubt the house in Fetter or Chancery Lane, lately mentioned, and the club was the Catholic Association.

the terms of a patron, or companion only, but rather in the character of a servant, or a steward in the apostolical ministry. He not only liberally supplied Father Parsons in all necessaries of life, of habitation, and travelling, with all altar requisites, but he begged with earnest entreaties to be allowed, at his sole expense, to do the same for Father Campion also, and the rest of their companions; nor was he more prompt in promising than munificent in performing. Nor was the bounty of this youth confined to the members of the Society of Jesus alone, but extended itself equally to other Priests and Catholics, in the bright hope of a heavenly recompense. He made his home a common asylum for Priests and Catholics, and it would often happen that, from the unexpected concourse, his house would be full, when he would give up his own bed and lie upon the ground. Nor did the rents of his estates long remain in his hands before some applicant for relief would require them, or else he would expend them in the service of the Church, in all which he consulted and followed the advice of Father Parsons. He would equip some of the Catholics with dress and money according to their age, more or less fine, and by enabling them to go about as gentlemen, or men of rank, with a gay appearance, especially such as were Priests. He assisted them in this way more than in any other, because, by concealing their real character, he enabled them, by this innocent stratagem, to elude the vigilance of the pursuivants and spies; and if ever the supply of clothing of this style fell short, he furnished them from his own back.

By his incredible liberality towards Catholics and Priests, especially towards the incarcerated, it is impossible to say how many souls he preserved from danger of ruin, and how many lapsed Catholics he caused to be restored to their faith. Indeed, so great were his labours for the help of souls in these kinds of works of charity, either personally, or by means of others, that they may be said easily to have exceeded in measure and merit those of any other Priest whatever. An intimate friend of his affirmed that a goodly volume might be filled with the names of the vascillating he strengthened, the lapsed he restored, and the tepid he aroused, by his own generous spirit, and especially young men his own equal in age and rank, out of whom, as we have seen, he formed the Catholic Association.

Early in July, 1580, as has been already mentioned in Mr. Pounde's Life, Father Parsons and Father Campion, duly equipped by George Gilbert, each having two horses and a servant, two suits of apparel for travelling, sixty pounds in money, with vestments, books, and everything needful for the church or for the road, rode forth from London, which was then emptied of friends and swarming with spies. Further stay there was both needless and dangerous, and hence they resolved, with the other Priests, to go forth on their appointed missions into the shires.

Father Parsons was accompanied by George Gilbert, Father Campion by Gervase Pierrepoint. They agreed to meet and take leave of each other at the house of a gentlemen at "Hogsdon" [Hoxton], probably that of Mr. Gardiner, the first convert of Father Parsons.

The Council soon knew of their departure from London, and sent pursuivants into most of the shires in England, with warrants to apprehend both of them wherever they could find them; but being diligently warned by the Catholics, they easily avoided their pursuers. "They lost their labour, and we had three or four months free to follow our business, in which period, by the help and direction of the young gentlemen that went with us, we passed through the most part of the shires of England, preaching and administering the Sacraments in almost every gentleman and nobleman's house that we passed by, whether he was Catholic or not, provided he had any Catholics in his house to hear us.

"We entered for the most part as an acquaintance or kinsfolk of some person that lived within the house, and when that failed us, as passengers, or friends of some gentleman that accompanied us; and after ordinary salutations, we had our lodgings, by procurement of the Catholics within the house, in some part retired from the rest, where, putting ourselves in Priest's apparel and furniture, which we always carried with us, we had secret conference with the Catholics that were there, or such of them as might conveniently come, whom we ever caused to be ready for that night late to prepare themselves for the Sacrament of Confession; and the next morning, very early, we had Mass, and the Blessed Sacrament ready for such as would communicate, and after that an exhortation, and then we made ourselves ready to depart again. And this was the manner of proceeding when we stayed least; but when there was longer and more liberal stay, then these exercises were more frequent."*

As one object of the present volume is to bring to light the dreadful sufferings inflicted upon Catholics by their Protestant brethren and countrymen, to compel them, though the attempts were vain, to embrace the new religion of Barlow, Cranmer, and Company, and to renounce the old Catholic traditions of their ancestors, we must pause a little to give some account of the labours of Father Parsons in his tour through the counties, accompanied by his faithful companion, George Gilbert, whose piety was not sufficiently satisfied by supplying riding-horses and men, who, whenever the Father went far from London to visit the country seats of the nobles, &c., would run before him through the country for many miles, giving notice to Catholics in what village or house they would find the Father on such a day, and in whatever neighbourhood he would visit on another day; but he himself would accompany him as a guide and passport, one time in his true character

* Father Parsons' manuscript Life of Father Campion. Stonyhurst MSS., quoted in Mr. Simpson's *Campion*, p. 164.

of a gentleman, at another just the opposite, as his servant and groom in livery, and, according to circumstances, a constant change of dress for both of them; for his great anxiety and heart-beating was entirely for the good Father's life; for his own he had no thought. Before giving a letter of Father Parsons from London, 17th November, 1580, to Father Agazzari, Rector of the English College, Rome, we will quote from one from a Priest in London, dated in July, 1581, to the same Father Agazzari, an extract from which, as regards the horrors of the prison of Wisbeach Castle, has been already given in the life of Thomas Pounde. "When a Priest comes to their houses, they first salute him as a stranger unknown to them, and then they take him to an inner chamber, where an oratory is set up, where all fall on their knees and beg his blessing. Then they ask how long he will remain with them, and pray him to stop as long as he may. If he says he must go on the morrow, as he usually does—for it is dangerous to stay longer—they all prepare for confession that evening. The next morning they hear Mass and receive Holy Communion; then, after preaching and giving his blessing a second time, the Priest departs, and is conducted on his journey by one of the young gentlemen;" that is, of the Catholic Association. The hiding-holes had become known by means of searchers and false brethren, by the middle of 1581; so that, even thus early, Catholics were compelled, when there was a night alarm, to betake themselves

L

to woods and thickets, ditches and holes. "Sometimes when we are sitting merrily at table, conversing familiarly on matters of faith and devotion (for our talk is generally of such things), there comes a hurried knock at the door, like that of a pursuivant; all start up and listen, like deer when they hear the huntsman. We leave our food, and commend ourselves to God in a brief ejaculation; nor is word or sound heard till the servants come to say what the matter is. If it is nothing, we laugh at our fright.

"No one is to be found in these parts who complains of the length of services. If a Mass does not last nearly an hour, many are discontented. If six, eight, or more Masses are said in the same place, and on the same day (as often happens when there is a meeting of Priests), the same congregation will assist at all. When they can get Priests they confess every week. Quarrels are scarce known amongst them. Disputes are almost always left to the arbitration of the Priest. They do not willingly intermarry with heretics, nor will they pray with them, nor do they like to have any dealings with them. A lady was lately told that she should be let out of prison if she would walk through a church. She refused. She had come into prison with a sound conscience, and she would depart with it or die. In Henry VIII.'s days, the father of this Elizabeth, the whole kingdom, with all its Bishops and learned men, abjured their faith at one word of the tyrant. But now, in his daughter's days, boys and women boldly profess the Faith before the judge, and refuse to make the slightest concession, even at the threat of death."*

The following is Father Parson's narrative of his missionary expedition with George Gilbert, as given in his letter of 17th November, 1580.†

"The heat of the persecution now raging against Catholics throughout the whole realm is most fiery, and such as hath never been heard of since the conversion of England. Gentle and simple, men and women, are being everywhere haled to prison, even children are being put into irons. They are despoiled of their goods, shut out from the light of day, and publicly held up to the contempt of the people in proclamations, sermons, and conferences, as traitors and rebels. It is supposed that the reasons of this great persecution are, first, the ill success of the English in Ireland, next, the demonstration made last summer against England by the Spanish fleet, and lastly, the coming of the Jesuits into the island, and the great number of conversions made by them, which has so astonished the heretics that they know not what to do or say. They are most troubled about a certain protestation of their Faith and religion, and of the reasons of their coming into England, which the Jesuits wrote and signed with their names, and placed in the hands of a friend, for fear that, if they were cast

---

* Mr. Simpson's *Campion*, quoting this letter, pp. 171, 172.
† Quoted in Simpson's *Campion*, pp. 172-4.

into prison, the heretics might pretend, as is their usual custom, that they had recanted. This protestation was communicated by the man who had charge of it to another, and by him to a third, and it soon came into the hands of an immense number, and even of the Queen's Councillors."*

"We hear that one month since more than fifty thousand names of persons who refused to go to the heretical churches were reported. Many more, I fancy, have been discovered since.

"The heretics, when they throw the Catholics into prison, only ask them one thing, to come to their churches, and to hear sermon and service. It was even lately proposed to certain noblemen to come, if it were only once a year, to church, making, if they pleased, a previous protestation that they came not to approve of their religion or doctrines, but only to show an outward obedience to the Queen; and yet all most constantly refused. A certain noble lady was offered her choice either to stay in prison, or simply to walk through the church without stopping there or exhibiting any signs of respect, but she declared that she never would. A boy of, I believe, twelve years of age who had been cheated by his friends into walking to church before a bride (as the custom here is), and had been afterwards blamed by his companions, was perfectly inconsolable till he found me a few days after, when he threw himself

* This was Father Campion's famous Challenge and Brag, as it was called. See a copy in Life of Mr. Pounde, part ii.

down at my feet, and confessed his sin. A thousand similar instances might be given.

"We, although all conversation with us is forbidden by proclamation, are yet most earnestly invited everywhere; many take long journeys only to speak to us and put themselves and their fortunes entirely in our hands. It is, therefore, absolutely necessary that more of our Society should be sent, if possible not fewer than five—one Spaniard, one Italian, and three Englishmen, who must be very learned men on account of the many entangled cases of conscience which arise, from no one here having ample faculties, and from the difficulty of consulting the Holy See—which is treason.

"There is immense want of a Bishop to consecrate for us the holy oils for Baptism and Extreme Unction, for want of which we are brought to the greatest straights, and unless His Holiness makes haste to help us in this matter we shall be soon at our wits end.

"The adversaries are very mad that by no cruelty can they move a single Catholic from his resolution, no, not even a little girl.

"A young lady of sixteen was questioned by the sham Bishop of London about the Pope, and answered him with courage, and even made fun of him in public, and so was ordered to be carried to the public prison for a woman of bad character.*

* Bridewell.

On the way she cried out that she was sent to that place for her religion, and not for immodesty.

"A certain English gentleman-pirate, lately returned with a booty of more than two millions, taken in the West Indies. The Spanish Ambassador reclaimed the spoil in the King's name, but the Queen gave the shuffling answer that the King of Spain had given harbour to the Pope's ships on their passage to Ireland. She asked, moreover, why the Pope, without being harmed, attacked her kingdom in this way. He answered that he rather wondered that the Pope did not attempt to do more against her who had treated him so abominably, not only in refusing him all his ecclesiastical rights, which from the most ancient times were allowed to the Holy See by the Kings of England, but also by libels, sermons, lewd pictures, and many other ways, by which his authority was defamed and brought into contempt. He said more to the same effect, and the Queen was silent then; but afterwards said to a nobleman that the Pope had written to her that he was prepared to approve the whole Protestant service, if she would restore him his title of Supreme Head of the Church. But in these parts there is often talk of these kinds of pretended letters.

"I keep myself safe here in London by frequent change of place. I never remain more than two days in one spot, because of the strict searches made for me. I am quite overwhelmed with business, to which I am obliged to devote the whole day, from early morning till midnight, after I have said Mass and Office, and preached, sometimes twice in the day. Therefore I hope for reinforcements, both from our Society and from the Pope's College.

"All Catholics here, lift up their hands and thank God and His Holiness for founding such a College at Rome, beyond all their hopes; and they beseech His Holiness, by the bowels of the mercy of our Saviour, to defend the College and to enlarge it for the needs of the present time.*

"Two days ago a Priest called Clifton was led in chains through the streets, and he walked with so cheerful a countenance that the people wondered. When he saw this he began to laugh heartily, at which the folks were still more struck, and asked him why he was the only one to laugh at his own sad case, for which everybody else pitied him. He answered, it was because he was the gainer in the business. In the beginning of this persecution there were some people in a certain county who were frightened, and promised to go to the Protestant church, but their wives stood out against them, and threatened to leave them if they, for human respect, left off their obedience to God and the Church. Many like things have taken place amongst boys, who for this cause have separated themselves from their parents."

* This was the English College, Rome, under the care of the Society of Jesus until 1773.

In October, 1580, Father Campion and Father Parsons returned towards London, to meet and confer once more, and to compare the results of their labours.

Father Parsons and his faithful friend, George Gilbert, reached London in the same month some days before Father Campion, for whom he tried to find a convenient lodging, but the persecution was become so hot and the search after him so close that it was thought unsafe for Father Campion to come to town. He therefore stayed at William Griffith's house, near Uxbridge, and here the meeting was held. Father Parsons' tour had been through the counties of Gloucester, Worcester, Hereford, and Derby. Father Campion had taken Berks, Oxford, and Northampton. In settling the plans for their next expedition it was resolved that Father Parsons should for the present remain in or near London, because he was not as yet so diligently sought for as Father Campion, whose protest or "brag" had kindled such a flame throughout the land, and was now in everybody's hands, furnishing almost the only topic at ordinary tables and public meetings. He had been asked for by the Norfolk and Lancashire Catholics, whom he had not reached on his first tour. Lancashire was fixed upon as the remotest from London and containing the greatest number of Catholics.

Whilst this conference was being held in Uxbridge, in October, 1580, a new proclamation, the third since the entrance of the Jesuits into England, was issued by the Council for their discovery and apprehension. This caused so great a difficulty in Father Campion's passage through the various counties towards the north, in consequence of the constables, pursuivants, searchers, and other catch-poles, that he was forced to stay more upon the way than he had purposed, and he took occasion of one of these enforced times of leisure to write to the Very Reverend Father General an account of his first tour.*

Following out the object of this volume, and especially seeing the close connection between the real subject of the history and Father Campion, who was furnished by him with the sinews for this desperate warfare, equally with Father Parsons, it is impossible to omit the present opportunity of introducing this very beautiful letter of that sweet and most glorious martyr. In fact it would rather seem that Mr. Gilbert accompanied Father Campion part of the way at least on his journey towards the north, after the meeting at Uxbridge. Finding himself more than ever beset, he was obliged, as we have just noticed, to tarry a long while on the way. "In fact," says Mr. Simpson, "I lost sight of him till about Christmastide, when Gervase Pierrepoint [one of Gilbert's Association, and who had accompanied Father Campion on his first tour] took him to

* Simpson's *Campion*, pp. 181, 182. Mr. Simpson also gives a copy of Father Campion's letter, from which the one presently given is taken.

the house of his brother, Henry Pierrepoint of Holme Pierrepoint and Thoresby, Notts, the ancestor of the Earls of Kingston; there he remained till the Tuesday after Twelfth Day, when he and his guide went to Mr. Langford, where they spent the Thursday and Friday; thence to Lady Fuljambes of Walton, Derbyshire, and thence to Mr. Powdrells of West Hallam, Derby, a famous resort, even a century later, of Priests, where they were joined by George Gilbert."* How long he remained does not appear, but Pierrepoint soon after returned, and then Mr. Tempest led Father Campion into Yorkshire. Mr. Gilbert's appearance at Mr. Powdrells' may only have been as a visit to Father Campion on some important matters relative to the undertaking. We may add here, that amongst the immense labours of Father Campion on his protracted and perilous journey to Lancashire, he stayed about twelve days at the house of Mr. William Harrington, of Mount St. John, brother-in-law of his guide, Mr. Tempest, during which time he was occupied in writing his famous book, *De Hæresi Desperata*, which afterwards appeared as his *Decem Rationes*. One of his host's six sons, William, was so struck by the conduct of the blessed martyr, that three years afterwards he fled over seas to Rheims, from whence in due time he returned to England a Priest, and himself suffered martyrdom at Tyburn also, February 18, 1594, for the Catholic religion.

* Simpson's *Campion*, p. 187.

Amongst Father Campion's marvellous escapes from the pursuivants, who were always upon his heels, was one at Mr. Worthington's house, Lancashire, where he was saved from seizure by a maid-servant, who, in affected anger, pushed him into a pond, and thus effectually disguised him, by covering him with mud.

The following is a copy of Father Campion's letter to Very Rev. Father General before referred to.

The first paragraph of the letter describes the passages of his career since his previous letter written from St. Omers *en route* to England, but it shall be given.

"Having now passed by God's great mercy five months in these places, I thought it good to give you intelligence by my letters of the present state of things here, and what we may of likelihood look for to come, for I am sure, both for the common care of us all, and special love to me, you long to know what I do, what hope I have, how I proceed. Of other things that fell before I wrote from St. Omers, what has sithence happened now I will briefly recount unto you. It fell out, as I construe it, by God's special providence, that tarrying for wind four days together, I should at length take sea the fifth day in the evening, which was the Feast of St. John Baptist, my peculiar patron, to whom I had often before commended my cause and journey. So we arrived safely at Dover the morrow following, very early, my little man and I together.* There we were at the very point of being taken, and were brought before the mayor of the town, who conjectured many things, suspected us to be such as indeed we were, adversaries of the new heretical faction, favourers of the old Fathers' faith, that we dissembled our names, had been abroad for religion, and returned again to spread the same. One thing he especially urged, that I was Dr. Allen, which I denied, proffering my oath, if need be, for the verifying thereof. At length he resolveth, and that it so should be, he often repeated that, with some to guard me, I should be sent to the Council. Neither can I tell who altered his determination, saving God, to Whom, underhand, I then humbly prayed, using St. John's intercession also, by whose happy help I safely came so far. Suddenly cometh forth an old man, God give him grace for his labour. 'Well,' quoth he, 'it is agreed you shall be dismissed; fare you well.' And so we two go apace. The whole thing considered, and the like that daily befall unto me, I am verily persuaded that one day I shall be apprehended, but that then when it shall most pertain to God's glory, and not before.

"Well, I came to London, and my good Angel guided me unwittingly into the same house that had harboured Father Robert [Parsons] before, whither young gentlemen came to me on every hand.† They embrace me, reapparel me, furnish me, service me,

* Brother Ralph Emerson, S.J.
† George Gilbert and his Catholic Association.

weapon me, and convey me out of the City. I ride about some piece of the country every day. The harvest is wonderful great. On horseback I meditate my sermon; when I come to the house, I polish it. Then I talk with such as come to speak with me, or hear their confessions. In the morning, after Mass, I preach; they hear with exceeding greediness, and very often receive the Sacraments, for the ministration whereof we are ever well assisted by Priests, whom we find in every place, whereby both the people is well served, and we much eased in our charge. The Priests of our country themselves, being most excellent for virtue and learning, yet have raised so great an opinion of our Society that I dare scarcely touch the exceeding reverence all Catholics do unto us. How much more is it requisite that such as hereafter are to be sent for supply, whereof we have great need, be such as may answer all men's expectation of them! Specially let them be well trained for the pulpit. I cannot long escape the hands of the heretics; the enemies have so many eyes, so many tongues, so many scouts and crafts. I am in apparel to myself very ridiculous. I often change it, and my name also. I read letters sometimes myself that in the first front tell news that Campion is taken, which, noised in every place where I come to, so filleth my ears with the sound thereof, that fear itself hath taken away all fear. My soul is in mine own hands ever. Let such as you send for, supply, premeditate and make count of this always. Marry, the solaces that are ever intermingled with these miseries are so great that they do not only countervail the fear of what punishment temporal soever, but by infinite sweetness make all wordly pains, be they never so great, seem nothing. A conscience pure, a courage invincible, zeal incredible, a work so worthy, the number innumerable, of high degree, of mean calling, of the inferior sort, of every age and sex.

"Here, even amongst the Protestants themselves that are of milder nature, it is turned into a proverb, that he must be a Catholic that payeth faithfully what he oweth, insomuch that if any Catholic do injury everybody expostulateth with him as for an act unworthy of men of that calling. To be short, heresy heareth ill of all men; neither is there any condition of people commonly counted more vile and impure than their ministers, and we worthily have indignation that fellows so unlearned, so evil, so derided, so base, should in so desperate a quarrel overrule such a number of noble wits as our realm hath. Threatening edicts come forth against us daily; notwithstanding, by good heed, and the prayers of good men, and, which is the chief of all, God's special gift, we have passed safely through the most part of the island. I find many neglecting their own security to have only the care of my safety.

"A certain matter fell out these days unlooked for. I had set down in writing by several articles the causes of my coming in, and made certain demands most reasonable. I professed myself to be a Priest of the Society; that I returned to enlarge the Catholic faith, to teach the Gospel, to minister the Sacraments, humbly asking audience of the Queen and the nobility of the realm, and proffering disputation to the adversaries. One copy of this writing I determined to keep with me, that if I should fall into the officers' hands it might go with me; another copy I laid in a friend's hand, that when myself with the other should be seized, another might thereupon straight be dispersed. But my said friend kept it not close long, but divulged it, and it was read greedily; whereat the adversaries were mad, answering out of the pulpit that themselves certes would not refuse to dispute, but the Queen's pleasure was not that matters should be called in question, being already established. In the meanwhile, they tear and sting us with their venomous tongue, calling us seditious, hypocrites—yea, heretics, too, which is much laughed at.* The people hereupon is ours, and that error of spreading abroad this writing hath much advanced the cause. If we be commanded, and may have safe conduct, we will [go] into the court.

"But they mean nothing less, for they have filled all the old prisons with Catholics, and now make new; and, in fine, plainly affirm that it were better to make a few traitors away than so many souls should be lost. Of their martyrs they brag no more now; for it is now come to pass that for a few

---

* For a copy of this famous protest, &c., see Life of Thomas Pounde, Esq., part ii.

apostates and coblers of theirs burnt, we have Bishops, lords, knights, the old nobility, patterns of learning, piety, and prudence, the flower of the youth, noble matrons, and of the inferior sorts innumerable, either martyred at once, or by consuming imprisonment dying daily. At the very writing hereof the persecution rages most cruelly. The house where I am is sad; no other talk but of death, flight, prison, or spoil of their friends. Nevertheless, they proceed with courage. Very many, even at this present, being restored to the Church—new soldiers give up their names, while the old offer up their blood; by which holy hosts and oblations God will be pleased, and we shall, no question, by Him overcome.

"You see now, therefore, Reverend Father, how much need we have of your prayers and Sacrifices, and other heavenly help, to go through with these things. There will never want in England men that will have care for their own salvation, nor such as shall advance other men's; neither shall this Church here ever fail so long as Priests and Pastors shall be found for their sheep, rage man or devil never so much. But the rumour of present peril causeth me here to make an end. Arise God. His enemies avoid. Fare you well. "E. C."*

* Mr. Simpson, in one of his very valuable notes, says (p. 376), "That he does not know where this letter is placed amongst the State Papers; that Mr. Lemon's Calend., 1547—1580, does not give it. It is either a contemporary translation of Campion's

To return again to Father Parsons and George Gilbert. After Father Campion's departure for the North they retired to London, where they found the persecution redoubled in vigour. A fourth proclamation came out against the Jesuits in November. Father Parsons was obliged to change his lodgings. Sometimes he lodged in Bridewell, sometimes in the suburbs, and sometimes even in one of the Queen's palaces. And from this time Catholics found their most secure asylums in the houses of pursuivants, or other civil or ecclesiastical officers whom they had in their pay. At this time Father Parsons procured the assistance of Mendoza, the Spanish Ambassador, who took him under his special protection, and would walk with him as one of his own men, whilst the Queen's officers were watching his house.*

well-known Epistle; or, if he wrote in duplicate, in English a well as in Latin, it may be his own English. It was probably written on the same day as Parson's letter, during the fifth month of his residence in England, reckoning from June 25. This would quite agree with November 17, 1580.

Since Mr. Simpson's work, viz., in October, 1872, another volume of the Calendars has been published by the indefatigable and talented Mrs. Green, the editor of so many of those essentially useful and important volumes, and to whom the public owes a great debt of gratitude. This volume is *Addenda*, 1580—1625, embracing all omitted matter between those dates, and amongst the rest this very letter. It may be found in *Dom. Eliz.*, State Papers, Addenda, Vol. xxvii., No. 60. It has no date, Mrs. Green puts 1580 (?); but Mr. Simpson most clearly accounts for the date November, 1580. The letter in the P. R. O. is only a copy. It has been compared with the one here given, the only difference being that the modern spelling has been used.

* Simpson's *Campion*, p. 183.

Several of Father Parson's friends had been captured—Ralph Sherwin, James Bosgrave, Hart, and others—and committed to prison. The danger was imminent, and, to add to it, Adam Squier, the son-in-law of Bishop Aylmer, whom we have already mentioned, and whose protection George Gilbert had purchased for Father Parsons, declared himself unable to carry out his agreement, because of the quarrels in which it involved him with the bishop, and the danger it exposed him to from the Council.

At this time Father Parsons was very busy in establishing a printing press by the aid of a young friend, Mr. Stephen Brinckley, one of the Gilbert Catholic Association, at a house called Greenstreet, East Ham, Essex, about five miles from London. But the danger increasing, Father Parsons with George Gilbert, fled away. The first book that issued from this press was probably (Mr. Simpson says) some book of devotions or encouragement to Catholics. After it was printed, the press was taken away. Afterwards, Father Parsons, at the house of another friend, Mr. Francis Browne, set to work to write his censure of Charke and Hanmer, in three parts. Here he incurred great trouble and risk in publishing the book, in consequence of the trap laid for Gilbert, whose bailiff had been ordered by the Council to come up to London to pay him his rents.

Father Parsons would not allow George Gilbert to go in person to receive them, but sent Browne and

Charles Basset (both of the Catholic Association) to Mr. Barnes' house in Tuttlefield, or rather to the house of one Higgins, an attorney. Whilst they were there, one George Cary came and seized both the money and the men.* Nevertheless, Father Parsons' "censure" appeared, and the quickness of its repartee made the Council doubly angry; and Father Parsons thinks that the proclamation of the 10th of January, 1581, ordering all young men to return from the foreign Seminaries, and denouncing all receivers and favourers of Priests and Jesuits, was a kind of reply to his "censure."†

Having thus traced the personal connection of George Gilbert with Father Parsons and Father Campion, as far as the means at hand will allow, we must now resume the thread of the narrative of his life.

He eluded indeed the ambuscades of the spies and pursuivants by a constant change of character and dress, as we have already seen. In all these

---

* This George Cary was the Queen's cousin, and once the intended husband of Mary Stuart. The holy martyr, Ralph Sherwin, having been seized and committed to the Marshalsea, like Father Campion (and we may add Thomas Pounde also), gave a general challenge to heretics to dispute with him. The gauntlet was taken up by Cary, who ordered certain questions to be put to him, but he afterwards shrunk from argument, and sent Sherwin to the Tower, with Father Thomas Cottam and others, 4th December, 1580 (Simpson's *Campion*, p. 183). This was a very conclusive *argumentum ad hominem*, and the usual one resorted to in those dark times.

† Simpson's *Campion*, pp. 185, 186.

dangers he never allowed himself to omit anything which he considered appertained to the greater glory and service of God, nor would he allow them to distract his mind in his prayers and meditations, and yet the dangers were never greater, and the searchers were tracking him in every direction, so that at last Father Parsons despaired of being able any longer to conceal him. The Privy Council, enraged at their unsuccessful attempts to catch him, had confiscated the greater part of his estates to the Treasury. Father Parsons, therefore, determined to send him to the Continent. Whilst waiting an opportunity for a vessel, he lay hid for some days by the seaside, in solitary and deserted caves, and the abodes of beasts, no slight hardship to a youth accustomed to every convenience and comfort of life. He spent this time in prayer with God, and his joy was so exuberant, that he seemed to taste somewhat of the delights of Paradise; and he afterwards related that he never felt more happy in his life than at that time. In fact, at this time no Catholic gentleman dared to offer to conceal him in his house, because, had he been found there, it would have cost them their own lives, so notorious had his virtues and merits rendered him.

In the month of May, 1581, he succeeded in crossing over to France, leaving Father Parsons seven horses for the necessary excursions of himself and other Priests in their constant searching after and serving the Catholics, especially amongst the higher class and nobles, who, for the greater part of the year, lived free in the country, and to confirm whom, under their severe trials, was so important an object. He also left him as much money as was in his power, not already confiscated to the Queen's Treasury, for publishing his many works *de Fide*, and for the promotion of piety and the consolation of Catholics.

The following is a copy of a letter written by Father Parsons to His Holiness, Pope Gregory XIII., by the hand of George Gilbert, whose final destination was to be the Eternal City.

"Beatissime Pater,—Although I hope your Holiness knows our affairs by other letters I have sent you, yet, as I have found a convenient messenger, to whom I must needs give some kind of letter, I wished to add some brief notice of our state. To-day the French Ambassadors have left London without having done their business, as is generally supposed, for the marriage is no longer talked about. We are daily expecting a fresh storm of persecution; for, two days ago, the Council sent an order to all parts of the realm, to make search for the Catholic recusants, as they call them, according to the form of a statute made in the last Session, which condemns every one above the age of sixteen to pay twenty pounds for every month they refuse to come to the Protestant church. And although there are very few Catholics who are rich enough to pay, and the rest must therefore expect to lie perpetually imprisoned, yet they are full of joy, and not at all anxious about this matter, as they hope that their case will be the same as that of the Israelites, and that the aggravation of their oppression will be the hope of a more speedy redemption.

"Against us they publish the most threatening proclamations, books, sermons, ballads, libels, lies, and plays. But the people receive us with the greatest eagerness, comfort us, and protect us. The number of the Faithful is wonderfully increased, and of our shrewdest foes we have softened many; some we have converted. The contest is sharp. God give us humility, patience, and fortitude! Whatever Priest or layman they lay hold of, whom they suspect to know anything about us, they torture on the rack to make him betray us; and quite lately they tormented one most atrociously, but could get nothing out of him.* Meanwhile, we live safely enough in their very sight. We talk, preach, write, and do everything else to resist them, expecting every kind of torment when we are taken; yet in the meantime, through God's goodness, we sleep soundly. We earnestly desire supplies of new men, and that soon, for fear we should be taken before they can take our places. So much concerning religious affairs.

"It now remains for me to tell your Holiness somewhat about the bearer of this letter, who, to tell the truth, is the chief cause of my writing. He is a

---

* This would have been, probably, a servant of Mr. Brinkley, lately mentioned, who was caught and racked, but nothing could be extracted from him (Simpson's *Campion*, p. 185).

young gentleman named George Gilbert, who has afforded the rarest spectacle to all England. He was a man of great wealth, a great favourite at Court, and devoted all his property to the defence of the Catholic religion. When we first entered the island, whilst others were in fear and doubt, he alone took us in, comforted us, clothed us, fed us, helped us with money, horses, servants, then took us about the island at his own expence; he journeyed with us, gave us books, and other necessaries, bought a press for us, sold some of his lands, and gave us a large sum of money for all purposes whereby the Catholic religion might be promoted; nor was this all, he bestowed continual alms on all the prisoners for religion, whereby he soon became so hateful to the heretics (especially as he had once been one of them), that they searched for him everywhere, and threatened to put him to a cruel death, if they could catch him. Now, although he cared little for this, yet since I saw that he could work no longer, nor stay in England, without plain peril of his life, and that we had more trouble and anxiety in protecting him than ourselves, I at last persuaded him to leave all things and cross over the sea, to keep himself for happier times. Now, therefore, I most humbly entreat your Holiness, or rather, all we Priests entreat you, because this one man was a most munificent patron to us all, that your Holiness will regard him, and console him for that consolation which he has given us, and whereby he has upheld the common cause.

For if we have done any good, a great part of it is to be attributed to this youth. So, if he finds an equal charity on that side, it will be a great edification for all, and no little encouragement to his companions to imitate his example.

"May the most merciful Jesus preserve your Holiness long, as all the Catholics here pray day and night, who think themselves so bound by the immense kindness you have shown, that they never cease talking of your Holiness, and to pray for your long life in this world, and your salvation and eternal happiness in the next.

"Your Holiness' most unworthy son,

"ROBERT PARSONS, S.J.

"London, 24th June, 1581."

George Gilbert was received at Rheims by Dr. Allen with all the love and veneration of an angel from Heaven. During the few weeks he remained with him, says the Doctor, he treated with me tenderly upon the affairs of his soul; and in sending him, and with him Charles Basset, who was one of his Catholic Association, and had also fled abroad from the storm of persecution at home, and was the worthy great-grandson of the noble confessor of the Faith and martyr, Sir Thomas More, the Lord High Chancellor of England, the victim of Henry VIII.'s passions, "These two young men," said he, "will be two great luminaries, shining resplendently there, as they have done in England." And in speaking of Mr. Gilbert in a letter to Father Agazzari, then Rector of the English College at Rome, of the 30th August, 1581, he says—"If any man of all the English nobility deserves well of the Seminarians, of the Fathers, of the Catholic religion, and of his country, it is this same most noble youth. There is no peril to which he has not been exposed. With a ready will and joyful heart he has suffered the plunder of his estates and fortune. Out of what remains to him he has been a large benefactor to the Catholics; also to us at Rheims, seeing the great poverty of our College, he has afforded no small relief—eighty golden crowns. And following his example, Charles Basset has done the same; which, for gentlemen in a strange land, exiles, and spoiled of their patrimony, was princely magnificence, or to speak worthily of them, was saintly charity."

The following is a copy of a letter which Dr. Allen wrote to the same Father Agazzari. The entire letter is given on account of its great interest, although the latter part only relates personally to our subject.

A copy of this letter is amongst the State Papers,[*] in Latin. Mr. Simpson gives the following translation.[†]

"We have heard from England, by a letter of Father Robert Parsons, S.J., that the persecution still rages with the same fury, the Catholics being

[*] State Papers, *Dom. Eliz.*, P. R. O., Vol. cxlix., No. 51.
[†] *Campion*, p. 208.

haled away to prison, and otherwise vexed, and the Fathers of the Society being most diligently looked for, but they are still, by God's singular providence, at liberty. One of them in the same chamber with Father Robert was, not long ago, seized and searched, but the Father was absent at the time. But a Mr. Briant who was a scholar of our College at Rheims, was not only taken, but twice most cruelly tortured on the rack, to make him tell where 'that Jesuit' was. But, so far from confessing anything of the sort, he laughed at the torturers, and though nearly killed with the pain, he said, 'Is this all you can do? If the rack is no more than this, you may bring a hundred more for this matter.'* The day after, John Nicholls, the apostate, met Father Tirrel, a scholar of your College, in the street and as soon as he saw him cried out 'Traitor,' and so took him; but he is not committed to the Tower, but to another prison called the Gatehouse, where he and Father Rishton, another pupil of your College, live happily. The Catholics were never more courageous, or more ready to suffer.

"Two days afterwards, a certain Mr. Ireson was taken with ten copies of our Apology; thus the book came to the knowledge of the Lords of the Council.

* This was the glorious martyr, Father Alexander Briant, S.J. He was seized April 28, 1581, suffering at Tyburn, December 1, 1581, æt. 28. For two years before his death he had determined to enter the Society of Jesus, and his desire was accomplished in prison. He endured worse than cannibal torture. Further notice of this great man must be reserved for a special history.

He is once again confined to his old home, the Fleet Prison, from whence he had by favour been delivered.

"The heretic, John Nicholls, boasts that he made a long oration at Rome before the Cardinals (nothing can be more false), which he has just published in his second book, and has at the same time promised to publish the former turned into Latin, with an appendix of his travels, in which he will explain at length the horrible murders and adulteries of the Catholics and the immoral life of the Jesuits and students. He now preaches publicly in London, but people are already universally tired of him, and I imagine that he will be soon tripped up, especially when the abjuration of heresies that he made at Rome in the Inquisition comes to England; for I have received the authentic copy of it which you sent, containing his whole recantation, and have sent it to Father Robert in England.

"Father Robert wants three or four thousand or more of the Testaments, for many persons desire to have them. He says that he earnestly hopes and expects more fellow-labourers of your Order; he says also that everything is going on well there, and that our Apology is vastly approved.

"I inclose a letter for the Holy Father, and another for our Protector, which you must see delivered to them. Therein I thank His Holiness for his many favours of this year, namely, for the foundation of the English College at Rome, for our College here provided for fifteen years, for his late extraordinary subsidy of five hundred golden crown, for assigning so good a protector to each College, and particularly, for not listening to the detractors of the Colleges and Missions, who, to excuse their own idleness and cowardice, assert that all these attempts on our country are in vain; and I show that it is sufficiently evident that these missions, and the endeavours of the Fathers and Seminarists are of extraordinary utility and finally, I assert and boldly pronounce, from the opinion, sense, and experience of all good men, that the Fathers and Priests have gained more souls this one year, in their own country, than they could possibly have gained in the whole world else, in the very longest lifetime. I write also that the dangers are not so great as to make it expedient to relinquish this duty, seeing that, of the fifty Priests (at least) who have this year been sent from the two Colleges, not more than ten have fallen into the enemies' hands, and up to this time the Fathers are altogether free, and labouring fruitfully. Lastly, we show that our books are thus moderately worded, and nothing brought forward in anger, but rather directed by pity, because of the vast utilty that accrues to every class of persons by reading them. So much for the letter to the Pope.

"But to our Protector, I merely write to beg him to turn his ears from certain idle and envious men, who say that the work of the Fathers and Seminarists in our country is useless. Moreover, I beseech him, for Christ's sake, not to forbid my sending five or six young men to that College next autumn, because ours has become so numerous, that we cannot anyhow feed them, although His Holiness has given us an extraordinary gift of five hundred gold crowns. So much for my letter to him. Note, that I am afraid to send any against his express injunction, lest we may seem to have no moderation, and to abuse the Pope's liberality too much. At this very time, we are obliged to send for twenty youths (for the most part gentlemen) from Douay to our own College here at Rheims, who otherwise would have to return to England, to the manifest damage of soul and body, since, on account of this proclamation, they can get no money from England. Moreover, within the last fortnight, more than twenty young men have come to me (poor me) from England, and where shall we get bread that these may eat, that each one of them may have only a little, lest they faint in this exile? May our Lord God bless and multiply our food!

"This week I have heard that the Fathers in England are not only well, but so occupied in the vineyard that they could not write to me. Father Campion is said to have published a Latin book of advice to the two Universities, but as yet it has not come to our hands. See, Father, whether or no they push the work forward. I have sometime ago sent them the letter of the Father General. May the Lord Jesus send many such labourers into His vineyard! At least thirty Priests have entered England since Easter, not one of whom was hindered on landing, or has since been taken, blessed be God. This year, I hope, will be every way a happy one for us. We sow in tears, but I trust in the Lord that we shall carry our sheaves with joy, through God, and this Pope Gregory, our true Father.

"I have with me, at present, the most generous companion and benefactor of the Priests in England, Mr. George Gilbert, who, on their account, has suffered the confiscation of almost all his goods and estates, and whom the heretics have personally persecuted more than the rest, knowing that the Fathers of the Society were kept and sustained by him. He has come hither into France, by the advice of Father Robert and others, in order to keep himself for *that time.** God willing, he will go to Rome in the autumn, and will dispose of himself according to the advice of the Father General and yourself. He tells me that more Fathers are very much wanted, if it were only to assist Father Robert, who, he says, has an incredible burthen to bear. He wrote those two beautiful little books himself, one of which we have hitherto supposed to be Campion's work. He preaches continually, he resolves cases of conscience for innumerable persons. The Catholics, in the midst of persecutions, have less scrupulous consciences than anywhere else that I know of, and have such an opinion of the Father, that they will not acquiesce in the judgment of any common Priest unless it is confirmed by Father Robert. He has seven men continually at work at a press, outside of

* *Ad illud tempus*—meaning, no doubt, for better times to dawn.

London (where the noise of the machine is less likely to betray it). He is continually appealed to by gentlemen, and by some of the Council, for necessary advice; so this Mr. Gilbert tells me, who has been his inseparable companion for this whole year, and who, at his departure, left Father Robert seven horses, for the necessary journeys and affairs of the Fathers and Priests, and a large sum of money to procure needful things, paper, types, ink, and the like, for great things can only be done at great expense, and for the success of such works we must have men who are not only despisers of money, but rich into the bargain.

"Father Campion is no less industrious in his own province, and it is supposed that there are twenty thousand more Catholics this year than last. Nor has God in this age anywhere given to the preachers of His word more power or success. Blessed be His Name for ever.

"Our Apology, as I hear, is read both by adversaries and friends, and the chief of the French mission has given it to the Queen to read. Christ Jesus, &c.

"Your Reverence's brother for eternity, as I hope,

both in earth and Heaven,

"WILLIAM ALLEN.*

"Rheims, June 23rd, 1581."

---

* There seems to be a little discrepancy in the dates of Father Parson's letter to the Pope, by Mr. Gilbert, which is dated 24*th June*, and Dr. Allen's dated 23*rd June*, when Mr. G. was at Rheims. This may be reconciled by the writers using the different styles, which would cause a difference of ten days.

George Gilbert then journeyed onwards to Rome, where, upon his arrival, he presented himself to the Very Rev. Father General, Claudius Aquaviva, S.J. The object of his journey was to place himself in the hands of his Paternity, to dispose of him in any way most *ad majorem Dei gloriam*, either by admitting him at once to the Society, which was his desire, or to defer his entrance, to the end that he might be more free to deal with the Holy Father and the Cardinals on matters relating to the affairs of religion in England, chiefly concerning Father Parsons and Dr. Allen, to which he applied himself with consummate prudence, and made himself exceeding useful. Father General Aquaviva willingly consented to this, and assigned him a room in the English College, where he lived, in the dress of a secular gentleman, a truly Religious life. He did not venture to move in any business unless it was first approved of by his Superiors, upon whose nod and judgment he would entirely depend, and this with so entire a submission of his own, that it could not be exceeded by the most humble and obedient Novice.

There were at that time English refugees in Rome, gentlemen once rich in their own country, but now, on account of their constancy in the profession of the Catholic faith of their forefathers, ruined and exiled. These afflicted ones found in George Gilbert an advocate, and, through him, a father in Pope Gregory XIII.; and when he was unable to assist any of them by means of others, he readily did so with his own as far as his circumstances permitted. Nor was he less solicitous in regard to their spiritual wants, putting them in mind, especially the higher classes, to conduct themselves, particularly before the criticising eye of the public, to the honour and credit of those holy Catholics of England, whose faith, piety, devotion, and every other kind of virtue was so distinguished, that thus Rome, by seeing their virtues reflected in themselves, would better understand what they found recorded of them in the pages of history. In like manner, amongst the young men of the College it is not easy to say what good he effected by his sweet and no less piercing discourses which were entirely of God and of spiritual things. But the most efficacious means, although silent, was the admirable example of his own life. As we have seen before, he had made a vow of chastity, and to preserve that angelical virtue immaculate, he was so jealous and guarded, that in passing through the city, in meeting women he would rivet his eyes firmly on the ground, and pass as far off as possible; and so shining was this rare virtue in him, showing itself in his virginal modesty, both of countenance, speech, and his whole gait and manner, that it bred a reverential love in the hearts of all towards him, as though he were an Angel in human shape. But he showed little respect towards himself, maltreating his body with that holy hatred which the Gospel lays down to be the true self-love of the soul. Continual and great were the penances with which he macerated his body. Whenever they were intermitted, the very reason for the omission reckoned as meritorious, because imposed upon him by holy obedience. Frequent were his fasts, and long his vigils every night. Twice a week he wore the rough haircloth; twice or thrice in the same time, severe and bloody disciplines, as might be seen after his death, these wholesome instruments of penance being found in shreds and stained with his blood. The two-fold cause of this holy severity against himself was, first, a purely penitential spirit in itself; and secondly, his great desire of martyrdom, long entertained, and so deeply rooted in his heart, that his withdrawal from England, in obedience to Father Parsons, had neither diminished his fervent desire nor his hope of being permitted some future day, if ever worthy of so great a grace, to obtain its glorious palm.

He often discoursed with the English students in the College upon the joys and glory of martyrdom, and these discourses were alike beneficial to both parties; to himself as a valve, as it were, for the escape of the flames of divine love that consumed him, whilst they tended to enkindle similar flames in theirs; although, on his part, he never discoursed with them upon this subject without many sighs, accusing himself as unworthy of this honour of martyrdom, in the immediate presence of which he had been for so long a time, and yet by his own faults and demerits could never attain to its palm. In the study and practice of prayer he was indefatigable;

and his unfeigned humility was such, that he would ever seek the lowest place in company, and the worst things in the community. He was most diligent in concealing his own good deeds, but could never say enough to load them upon others. When he heard his own merits and sufferings for the Faith in England recorded, if he could not otherwise turn the subject of conversation, so great was his confusion of face and the pain it caused him, that to save him from the suffering the company would at once turn to another topic.

He would spend five hours a day in prayer, and, when disengaged from business, a much longer time in spiritual exercises, in examining the resolutions made, and in reflections upon divine things pondered over in his last meditation; and he made daily notes and memoranda in writing. He would then also renew with greater instance a petition he was accustomed daily to make before the Blessed Sacrament, which was for one of two favours, whichever might be most agreeable to the will of God, (and both were granted to him, as we shall see further on), to die in some important service for the Holy See and religion, and in the Society of Jesus; which Order, the more he meditated on the life of our Saviour, so much the more he felt his love and desire for it increase, because in its whole institute and rules, its manner of life, its labours, its bulwark of holy obedience, &c., he saw that it so closely followed the divine model of Him Whose name it bears, and he felt that to himself, already despoiled of all his goods for the Catholic faith, and of all carnal delights by his vow of chastity, it only remained to consecrate to God, in the Society of His Son, all that was left him, his understanding and will, the accomplishing of which is the special office of holy obedience.

In his labour after this gain of virtues he was most remarkable. He conformed himself to the rules and regulations of the College just as one of the *alumni*, and so strict was he in the least point, that, although himself, for want of habit, not so very ready in the Latin tongue, he would, when addressed in English, respond only in Latin, such being the custom of the College. So compliant did he show himself to the least nod of the Father Rector and his advice, that he seemed to be divinely taught in this science of holy obedience. The very mention of it was enough to make him quaff off the most repugnant and nauseous physic in his sickness with alacrity. Having on one occasion promptly done this, he said familiarly to a certain Father, "I am in great glee, my Father." Being asked the cause of his great joy, he replied, "The most Blessed Virgin showed herself to me on this occasion with a serene and benevolent countenance, whereas a short time since she looked upon me with a severe one, because on a certain occasion I clung too much to my own will."

Whilst the students of the College were quietly

sleeping at night he would secretly retire to the church, and there, kneeling before the most Divine Sacrament, would pray for a long time. The same also he would do in the day time; and he allowed no hour to pass wherein he did not raise his mind and heart to Heaven, especially in transacting business, when he would hold frequent colloquies with God, using for this purpose chosen verses out of the Psalms. He also daily recited the solemn Office of the Blessed Virgin; but otherwise, applying himself solely to mental prayer, he did not make so much use of vocal. On each Sunday and festival he received the most Divine Body of Christ, mingled with sighs and tears of tender devotion, which, in spite of his efforts to suppress, would openly break forth. He would make the favourite devotion of the visit to the seven great Basilicas of Rome—St. Peter's, St. Paul's, St. Sebastian's, St. Laurentius', Santa Croce, St. Mary Major's, and St. John Lateran's—at least every fortnight; and this alone, in order without distraction, to treat with God and the Heavenly Court.*

He was accustomed to say that in prayer we should persevere, using a holy violence with God, as Jacob did, saying to the Angel, "I will not let thee go, unless thou bless me"—*Non dimittam te, nisi benedixeris mihi;* and that when he prayed thus, *Hinc ego Domine non recedam, nisi id quod postulo, vel certè nisi firmam impetrandi fiduciam dederis*—"I will not,

---

* A circuit involving some ten miles at least.

O Lord, depart hence unless Thou wilt either grant me now what I ask, or else a firm confidence of obtaining it."

His only subjects of meditation were upon the life and death of Christ, declaring that from these he enkindled twin desires—the one to embrace every opportunity of expending his labours, his blood, and his life in the service of our holy Mother the Church, and the salvation of souls; the other, of entering the Society of Jesus, considering it, as before mentioned, so agreeable to the model of the life of our Lord, so intent only upon the salvation of souls and the good of religion, even to the lavishing of life. He desired that all the meditations of the *alumni* should turn upon these three points—the life and death of our Lord, on the glory and gains of martyrdom, and on examples taken from the Saints. He would frequently wander in thought through the various orders of the Heavenly host, and saluting in familiar colloquies one while this, another while that Saint, he would demand of them by what means, and by the exercise of what virtues, he could attain to their so great glory; and, as though he heard their answers, he would incite himself to the endeavour of imitating them. For instance, "Thou, O St. Stephen! whence do I see you adorned with a crown of such resplendent jewels!" And St. Stephen would seem to answer, "These are the stones with which, since the Jews crushed me, the Blood of Christ has brilliantly polished for me." "And thou, O St. Bartholomew!

whence comes that triumphal purple robe wherewith thou art mantled?" "It is my skin, which I willingly parted with for my Lord Christ." "And thou, O St. Francis! by what means didst thou obtain a throne so sublime, as though thou hadst found riches?" "This is the fruit of poverty which I preferred before all earthly riches and delights." And this kind of colloquial prayer he recommended also to the students of the College, as most apt to incite them cheerfully to bear labours.

His great desire of martyrdom produced a corresponding devotion to the martyrs. And hence, amongst his other benefactions, says Bombinus, he covered the walls of the church of the English College in Rome with the pictures of the English martyrs, in which he went to great expense; but the painting, the subject, and the order of the whole thing, he left to Father William Goode, who at that time was the English confessor in the College. The Annual Letters of the English College, 1583, say that these martyrs included all from the first conversion of England. Father Bartoli says that Mr. Gilbert gave to the same church of the English College the painting of St. George the Martyr, Patron Saint of England, and his own Patron, whose history is represented in the Church, and this work he himself superintended; and if the artist succeeded in producing a picture so to the life, it was due to George Gilbert's constant watching him till the work was finished.

In the meantime, the holy Pontiff Gregory XIII. frequently summoned Mr. Gilbert to his presence upon a matter of business, which was generally believed was one of high import to the interests of the Catholic religion, in the transacting of which it was necessary for him to go to France, though it was currently believed that his journey really tended towards England.

Whilst he was preparing to execute this commission with all possible despatch, the very day before he should have mounted his horse to depart, it pleased God that he should be seized with a fever so violent as to carry him off in seven days; in which brief space many remarkable things were observed in him exhibiting proof of his deep devotion and piety, and of edification to the whole College.

In being carried on his bed to another chamber more convenient, passing by the door to the church, he begged the bearers to carry him inside ; for which, permission being obtained, he became so completely absorbed in God that nothing but an order of obedience from the Father Rector, who was called in on purpose, could induce him to consent to be removed. Lying on his bed, he esteemed nothing so grievous as that he was departing this life like a sluggard (to use his own words) in bed. Hence he ardently desired that his life might be spared for this end only—to consummate it by a violent death in the defence of the Catholic religion. But on the Father Rector telling him that such was not the wil of God, and desiring him to turn his mind for the short moment left him to God and spiritual things, he immediately became calm and resigned, and henceforth banished from his heart all thoughts and desires of a longer life.

Having received the consolation of the last Sacraments of Holy Church, Extreme Unction and Viaticum, and beholding the students of the College who surrounded his bed, and by whom he was so singularly beloved, weeping and showing uncontrolled signs of affliction at this rapid and premature death of so distinguished a youth; "Cease those tears," he said, "it rather befits *me* to weep, who alone am most wretched of all, being thus taken away without shedding my blood." And then, addressing each one singly according to their various dispositions, to one he said, "What have *you* to weep for, for whom may be reserved chains and prisons?" "Why *you*," he said to another, "who may have to endure scourgings and fetters, and to whom is still left the full hope of martyrdom, whilst I, who for two years was panting after it, and often close upon it, die this sluggish death in bed?" Then taking in his hands the wooden crucifix which the blessed martyr, Father Alexander Briant, had carved for himself for the purpose of animating his desire of dying that dreadful death at Tyburn for his Lord, he exclaimed, "O cross, O rope, O sword, O most desirable death, why was I, wretched man, unworthy to enjoy you, and through you to pour out my blood? Who will give me to

be treated with the treatment of these holy martyrs? O most beloved, most venerated Sherwin and Briant, aid me by your prayers that I may obtain pardon for my sins, which exclude me from so great a favour, and cause me to die here idle. Who will give water to mine head and a fountain of tears to mine eyes?"*
He then began to address the blessed martyr, Father Campion, his former most affectionate friend, familiarly as though present, greatly lamenting his lot that he was not found worthy to be his companion when dragged on the hurdle to Tyburn gallows.† Then when he had offered to Christ our Lord, the sweetest Son of the most Blessed Virgin Mother, the merits of His most holy Passion, and the sorrows that most blessed of mothers endured in life, with the excess of joy wherewith she was flooded at her death, and begging the prayers of his good Angel Guardian, and his Patron Saint, for protection in the awful passage, he offered himself as an holocaust to God, and begged of Very Reverend Father General Claudius Aquaviva to admit him to the Society of Jesus he so greatly

---

* "Quis dabit câpiti meo aquam, et oculis meis fontem lacrymarum?" etc. In Bishop Kennett's Collection, vol. iv., lviii., Lansdowne MSS., No. 982, British Museum, in "some additions to Mr. Wood's account of Alexander Briant," it is stated that "Alexander Briant had shaved his crown himself, and made him a crosse of a peece of a trencher, which he held in his hand openly, and prayed to; which, when he was rebuked for, he boldly and stoutly made answer that his crowne was of his own shaving, and he had good hope to doe it againe."

† The print at the commencement of this Life represents the above scene, with Father Campion appearing to him.

loved and honoured, and for which, as Bartoli observes, he could not have done and suffered more had he always been a member of it; and as a last request that he might be buried in the Church of St. Andrea, the church of the Roman Novitiate, his voice became feeble. At that moment the Father Rector Agazzari, who had gone to the Gesù to obtain from the Father General the necessary leave and faculties to admit him to the Society, and the vows of religion, returned to the College and imparted to him the joyful news. Returning hearty thanks to God, the Master of all vows, exerting himself he pronounced the formula of the vows with a most ardent affection of love, and then uttering the most holy names of Jesus and Mary, and in fervent colloquies with God, closing his eyes as one asleep, he rendered up his happy soul into the hands of his Creator at the fourth hour of the night, on the 6th of October, 1583. At first the bystanders thought he was sleeping, but when they saw that he was really dead, they kissed his hands and feet, bathing them with their tears.

Being well known at the Court of Rome as a man of distinguished virtues, his loss was there deeply regretted, so much so that the Sovereign Pontiff, Gregory XIII., himself, who so fully appreciated both his virtues and his talents, was deeply grieved at his premature death, declaring it to be a great loss to England. He was carried to the Church of St. Andrea, and there buried amongst the novices, according to his desires and the wish of the Father General.

He left a legacy of eight hundred scudi to the Novitiate of St. Andrea, which Very Reverend Father General gave to Dr. Allen towards the heavy expenses of his College at Rheims. The following is an extract of a letter from his Paternity to Dr. Allen dated 10th October, 1583.* After relating the holy death of George Gilbert, and expressing the good hope they had that being now in Heaven he would much more successfully promote the affairs of the Catholic religion in England than before, he adds, "Besides this, the same Mr. George, who as he long ago, and especially at the close of his life, devoted himself to our Society (a fact well known to your Reverence), and on this account wished to be buried in the church of the Novitiate of St. Andrea; so for the relief of the poverty and needs of that house he has left by his will, eight hundred scudi. Which charity and benefaction, although most gratifying to us, nevertheless, considering the great needs of England, we believe it will be to the greater honour and service of God to employ the whole for the benefit of that nation. I therefore consider that it may be more useful for your Reverence at Rheims to employ it for your College, or else to relieve the poverty of some afflicted English exiles, or to form a fund towards

* Quoted by Father Bartoli, *Inghil.*, l. iv., p. 76. "Nel registro di Francia," October 10, 1583.

the support of some that would live in Rome. It remains for your Reverence to determine, and whatever course you deem best shall be willingly executed."

To save confusion in the narrative, the following papers relating to Mr. Gilbert, copied from the State Papers, P.R.O., are added at the end.

Dom. Eliz., Vol. 140, No. 62.

"The Examination of John Taylor, taken before me, George May, 26th December, 1580.

"1. To the first question he sayeth he remembreth not that he hath seen him, George Gilbert, these four or five monthes, but that one of his servants coming from Bedford mett with him and his servant, Roger Yardley als Caules, early betwixt St. Talbons [St. Albans] and London, about a month sins. His servant hath sins bin at the house of this examinant, who asked him whether his master was in towne; he answered no; he asked farder whither he rid at the time he was met withall by Saynt Talbons; he answered 'to his frendes,' but told not whither; he demanded farther when he wold com to towne, and where he wold lye when he came: he answered that shortly he wold be in towne, but knew not wher he determined to lye: this communication was betwixt a fortnite and three weekes last past, betwixt the said Roger and this examinant.

"2. To the second he sayeth that in the towne he knoweth not directly the haunts; but at Mr. Townsend's in Barbican, and as he thinketh, at Mr. Roper's, in Shen [Shire] Lane, and at one Cook, a sadlers, in Flete Street, and to Sir Thomas Jarets [Gerard], and to the Master of the Rowles professing, and to Mr. Allington, one Norris, sometimes of the Inns of Court, and ye ij Roscarochs: (the said Townsend hath a taylor, one Thomas, that served Mr. Gilbert halfe a yere sins): in the country he resorteth to his tenant's houses in Bucks, for thereabouts, he thinketh, his mother, Grace Gilbert, a widow, dwelleth (he farther sayeth that this Gilbert hath bin a very earnest Protestant about seven years past). Also about Nottingham towne, as he thinketh, Sir Gervase Clifton's. His most familiar frendes, to his knowledge, be one Mr. Perpoynt, lying in Nottinghame; also one Mr. Peter Baset, one that lyeth much at Mr. Roper's; one Mr. Rob. Gifford, of Stafford; one Brinkley; and divers others, which this examinant remembereth not nor knoweth.

" 3. To the third, he sayeth Roger doth use chiefly to Yardley, a miller at Stetbridge, both because he is akin to him and a mayde in the house cauled Winefrid, where this examinant ij day sens, asking for Roger Yardley, sayd that he thought he wolde within a day or ij write letters to one Offal; where Mr. Offall did lye he knew not: demanding further wher Mr. Gilbert was, he answered that he was ignorant thereof.

" 4. To the fourth, he sayeth he knoweth none of them by those names, but he will inquire of his wife, whether any such did resort to his house or not.

"5. To the fifth, he sayeth that he is of resonable tawle stature, brode sholdered, with a big leg bending somewhat in the knees, short visaged, fayre complexioned, resonable well coloured, litell here [little hair] uppon his face, and short if he have any, thik of speech, and about twenty-four years of age.

"6. To the sixth, he sayeth he will most faythfully perform theyr commandments, if it shold be for his owne father. He sayeth farder, that about half a year sens, Norris the Pursuivant, as he thinketh, brought Gilbert before the Bp. of London, but how from thence he was discharged he knoweth not, but Norris told this examinant that he was an honest gentleman, and well might he saye so.*

"JOHN TAYLOR."

* Mr. Simpson, in making an extract from the above State Paper in his *Life of Campion*, p. 211, adds, that about Midsummer, 1510, Mr. Gilbert was taken before Aylmer, the Protestant Bishop of London, by Norris the Pursuivant, but discharged on Norris declaring him an honest gentleman. Norris might well say so, for Gilbert paid him liberally, and hired his house to be a kind of sanctuary for hunted Recusants, as we have already seen.

Mr. Townsend, of the Barbican, was probably either Isaac Townsend or his brother Rob. Townsend, of Ludlow, both brothers of George Gilbert's mother. Robert had been Mr. Gilbert's guardian till he came to the age of eighteen, when he delivered him his lands and his free marriage, before which time his uncle kept him as a scholar at his own house, and after at the University. Mr. Gilbert, however, now scarcely ever visited his said uncle, a Protestant, and never stayed more than three days together (See the Examination of Townsend).

Dom. Eliz., 1581, Vol. cxlviii., No. 11.

"Chester. [Sir Wm. Gerarde and Sir G. Caulneley (Sheriff of Chesh.) to Earl of Leicester.]

"Yt may like yr honors yesterday, the second of this month, wee received your honourable letter of the xxviiith of Feb. last, comytting thereby to our diligent and secret travell the apprehension of Campion the Jesuit, who, as yt was informed, and one Gilbert, were conveyed by one Townsend of Ludlow, whose cozen the same Gilbert ys, to Mr. Rafe Duttons of Hatton, who hath married ye said Townsend his sister.

"The same afternoon I, the sheriffe, with some fewe of my own servants and a coople of gentlemen sent by me from Chaunccllor Woode to Hutton, where we found Mr. Button, the same Townsend of Ludlowe called Roburt, and a younger brother of his named Isaac. Presenthe I, the sheriffe, delt with Mr. Dutton, touchinge his knowledge of this Campion, who I was assured would tell me his knowledge. I founde he never either knewe or heard of the man, and the younger Townsend made the like answer. Wee told the said Townsend of Ludlow that the surmyse made was that he should be the conveyor of Campion and his nephew Gilbert to Hutton. He utterly denyed to have any knowlledge either of the purpose or that his cozen Gilbert had any dwelling with him. After this deniall, and upon dewe search made in the house, where wee found no person other then ye ordinarye howsehould of ye same Mr. Dutton and the servants of ye said Townsend, we departed, having taken order for our meeting at Chester in the morning, at which tyme chiefly, at the request of the said Rob. Townsend himself, wee examined him upon his othe upon the materialest parts of the matters contiyned in the said letter, whereof the suspicion was gathered. His answer upon his oathe subscribed by him & us, wee send to your honor inclosed; which although of our own knowledge wee cannot afferme, yet upon other circumstances falling out upon the taking of the examination, wee be in oure conceyvings fully resolved that he speaketh trewly.

"We found that the said Townsend had the wardshipp of this Gilbert his sister's sonne, that when he came to the age of xviii. years he delivered him his lands and his free marriage, before which tyme Townsend kept him as a schollar at his owne house, and after at the Universitye. That sithen he, ye said Gilbert, had charge to fynde himself, he seldom came to his vncle, and at his coming made noe long aboade. And that he lastly came to him about mydsomer last with one mann, and tarryed about three days; and otherwise, then at those comyngs, he seldom saw his said cozen. Denying upon his oath to know where he now is, or hath been sithen he departed, but judged he was travelled beyond the seas. Upon the taking of which exam. we took order for appearance of the said Townsend at any tyme before yr honors, and returned him to

o

Hutton. And soe, having at full advertized your honors of the manner of our proceedings, wee take leave.

"At your honorable commands,

"GEO. CAULNELEY,

"WM. GERRARD.

"Chester, the 4 of March, 1580 (1)."

"The exam. and declaration of Robert Townsend, Esquier, taken before us, Sr. Wm. Gerrard and Sir Geo. Calveley, Kts., the 3rd of March, 1580, upon his corporall oathe.

"Examined when he last saw his nephew, Geo. Gilbert. Saith, about midsomer last past, the same Geo. came to him and tarried three or foure daies or thereabout, and after departed.

"Examined what company the said Geo. had with him at his coming thither. Saith his own man, one Roger, and noe stranger.

"Examined whether he saw the said Gilbert at any tyme sithen. Saith he did not to his knowledge.

"Examined whether he, this examin! doe knowe or have seene one Edmund Campion the Jesuite. Saith upon his oath, to his knowledge, he never sawe him, neyther at this howre doth he know him of all men.

"Examined whether he found out upon talk with Gilbert that Gilbert dyd knowe the same Campion.

Saith that he could not perceyve at any time by any speach that Gilbert and Campion were acquainted.

"He utterly denieth upon his oath that he knoweth eyther the sayd Campion or knoweth where he now ys, or ever was to his knowledge, what company the said Gilbert hath kept with the said Campion, whether they have been in company, or whether the said Campion have any maintenance by the sayd Gilbert, or upon what occasion the sayd Gilbert shoulde extend any favour to the sayd Campion, he knoweth not himself, nor by the report of the sayd Gilbert.

"ROBERT TOWNESHEND.

"WM. GERRARD,

"GEO. CAULNELEY"

Book the Third.

FATHER THOMAS DARBYSHIRE, S.J

FATHER THOMAS DARBYSHIRE, S.J.

FATHER THOMAS DARBYSHIRE was nephew to Bonner, the Catholic Bishop of London, who, when Queen Mary, on the death of the boy-King, Edward VI., assumed the reins of government, was conspicuous for his zeal in arresting the hitherto hidden serpent of heresy; but what is of greater importance, he was a disciple and imitator of the heroic fortitude of that Prelate, who was not to be moved or shaken, either by the feigned promises or the real threats of Queen Elizabeth, who, in punishment of his invincible firmness in the Catholic faith, and obedience and submission to the Sovereign Pontiff, condemned him to be buried alive in a most wretched and painful dungeon, there to be slowly consumed by a long martyrdom of suffering, to which he at last succumbed. Bishop Bonner employed Father Darbyshire as his chancellor in the administration of his episcopal functions, and made him his fellow-soldier in combating the enemies of the Faith.

He was educated at Broadgate Hall, Oxford, where he completed the degree of Doctor of the Civil Law,

17th February, 1555. Afterwards taking Orders, he was made Doctor of Canon Law, as also of Divinity. Having qualified himself in this manner, and supported by his uncle's interest, he had considerable benefices and dignities bestowed upon him. He was successively made Archdeacon of Essex, Canon of St. Paul's, Chancellor of the Diocese of London, and lastly, Dean of St. Paul's.* Queen Mary's death, and with that event the overthrow of the Catholic religion in England, put a stop to his further promotion. He was conspicuous for his constancy in defending the Faith on the accession of Elizabeth, and being, in consequence, deprived of all his preferments, dignities, and ample fortune, which, by the favour of his Princes and of the Holy See, and in reward of his talents and learning, had been bestowed upon him, he remained still in England for some time longer, in hope of seeing another change. He was held in great esteem amongst the Catholics in England, and was deputed in their name to the assembled Fathers of the Council of Trent, to procure their opinion upon a point of controversy, then much agitated amongst the English Catholics, whether they were permitted to frequent the churches and services of the Protestants, to which they were forced under pain of the severest penalties. He shortly returned to England, having procured their opinion, to the effect that so to attend

* Father Bartoli, *Istoria S.J. Inghil.*, says that he was Professor of Philosophy in the Academy of the "Sapienza," of London.

the said churches and worship would be a grave sin. Dr. Oliver, in his notice of Father Darbyshire,* says that through his zealous representations, the Fathers of the Council of Trent passed their decree, *De non adeundis hæreticorum ecclesiis.*

In the following paper, of which an extract is made, and which is supposed by the editor of the *State Paper Calendar* to date about 1561, Father Darbyshire is named Doctor Darbyshire, &c. A rather full extract is given, being a curious document, and showing the spirit of the times, and the active zeal of the new pseudo-bishops, on stepping into the sees of the ejected orthodox ones.

State Papers, *Dom. Elizabeth*, Addenda, Vol. xi., No. A 5, 1561 [?]

"Schedule signed by Edmund [Grindall], Bishop of London, Richard [Cox] of Ely, William [Downham] of Chester, and three others, Commissioners of Recusants who are at large, &c.

"List of evil disposed persons of whom complaint has been made, but who lurk so secretly that process cannot be served upon them [*inter alios*]—

"Philip Morgan, late of Oxford.

"Friar Gregory, a common Mass sayer.

"One Ely, late Master of St. John's College, Oxford.

"Dr. Robinson, late Dean of Durham, is excused by his lameness. One thought to do much hurt in Yorkshire.

* *Collect. S.J.*

"One Morris, late chaplain to Dr. Bonner, wanders about Staffordshire and Lancashire very seditiously, and is the person who cast abroad the seditious libel in Chester.

"Robert Gray, Priest, much supported at Sir Thomas Fitzherbert's, and now wandering in like sort. A man meet to be looked to.

"Dr. Hoskins, late of Salisbury, a subtle adversary, through the example of Sir Thomas Fitzherbert, John Sacheverell, and John Dracot, committed by us to prison, and through their families and friends, most in the counties of Stafford and Derby, are evil intended to religion, and use froward speeches in ale houses."

"List of persons who have fled over the seas [*inter alios*]—

"Dr. Bullock, late Prebendary.

"Dr. Darbyshire, late chancellor to Dr. Bonner, and his kinsman.

"William Taylor, late chaplain to Archbishop of York."

"Prisoners in the Fleet, by order from us [*inter alios*]—

"Sir Thomas Fitzherbert, Knt.

"Dr. Scott, late Bishop of Chester.

"Dr. Harpesfilde, late Archdeacon of London.

"Thomas Wood, late Parson of High Ongar, Essex, and chaplain to Queen Mary.

"Dr. Cole, late Dean of St. Paul's.

"Prisoners in the Marshalsea—
"Doctor Bonner, late Bishop of London.
"John Symes, a Priest of Somersetshire."

"In the Counter, Poultry—
"John Dracot, gentleman."

"In the Counter, Wood Street—
"John Sacheverell.
"Thomas Atkinson, clerk, late Fellow of Lincoln College, Oxon.
"John Greete, a Priest, late beneficed in Hants."

"In the King's Bench—
"John Baker, clerk, late Parson of Stamford Rivers, Essex."

Although Father Darbyshire is returned in the above amiable list of the three Right Reverend Fathers in God, as fled beyond seas, it is most probable that he was simply gone on the above embassage to the Fathers assembled at the Council of Trent.

At length the Protestants perceiving that many by Father Darbyshire's example and authority retained their faith with constancy, and that many more were converted by him from heresy, he was seized and condemned to a most wretched prison. Here, on one occasion when deeply oppressed by his sufferings and sorrows, and weeping over his misfortunes, an image of the Crucified Saviour of the world suddenly appeared to him, bleeding, and, as it were, affixed to the wall, which before that time he had never observed.* By this vision he was so strengthened to undergo all events, even death itself, that from that moment, he had no other desire than for the rack, the tortures, the axe, and the gibbet itself. But instead of death, being banished for life, grieving at having the laurels of martyrdom thus torn from his brow, he determined, deeming it an honour to do so, to accomplish this desire of martyrdom, by embracing one of a chaste and Religious life in the Society of Jesus—a martyrdom no less severe because more prolonged. He did this the more willingly having been frequently connected with that holy name, for, by order of Philip and Mary he had been appointed by royal commission the Prefect of a certain Sodality called by the name of Jesus, to which Sodality belonged the distribution of large alms. And not long after this he was unanimously voted as Principal of another College of Priests, called "The Table of Jesus," in the room of the deceased Suffragan of London. He expressed his feelings at being chosen to such great benefices, and afterwards to the Society of Jesus, in these words— *Qui me prius promoverat ad Fraternitatem* Nominis Jesu; *qui secundo ad mensam* Nomini Jesu *invitarat; tertio quoque in* Societate Nominis Jesu *collocavit; fecit mihi magna qui potens est, et sanctum nomen ejus—* "He hath done great things to me, and holy be His

* The print at the head of this Life represents this scene.

See page 223.

name, Who first promoted me to the Confraternity of the *Name of Jesus;* Who secondly invited me to the *Table of the Name of Jesus;* and thirdly Who hath also placed me in the *Society of the Name of Jesus.*"

He was no less delighted to join the Society of Jesus on account of its holy name than of his admiration of its Institute. When during his deliberations as to the choice of a state of life, he was hesitating, being mainly anxious of securing his own personal salvation, and had turned his thoughts towards the recluse mode of life of the severe and holy Order of the Carthusians, a stranger suddenly stood before him, the door being shut, and thus addressed him—"And thou," said he, "by becoming a Carthusian, consultest indeed thine own salvation; but what becomes of thy neighbours?"—*Et tu (inquit si), Cathusianus futurus es, saluti tuæ consules, at ubi futurus est proximus.* This apparition and address banished all further hesitation, and he recognized it as a finger pointing to the Society of Jesus, which specially devotes itself both to its own and its neighbour's salvation. Thereupon he betook himself to Father Laynez, who was at that time attending the Council of Trent as one of the Pope's theologians, and who succeeded St. Ignatius, as second General of the Society, on the death of the former, July 31, 1556.

Being sent by Father Laynez to Rome, he was there received into the Society 1st May, 1563, then aged forty-five. Mr. Dodd says that he had first visited several parts of France and Flanders, and that after his reception into the Society his time was chiefly spent in catechising youth in the Colleges, which his facility in the Latin tongue enabled him to perform with great success, and that Dr. Allen, the founder of Douay College and afterwards of the English College at Rheims, had a great respect for him, and meeting him at Rome, they came down together to Rheims where they arrived April 2, 1580, and that subsequently on Father Darbyshire being obliged to leave Paris on account of his bad health, and for change of air, Dr. Barret, being then President of the College at Rheims, invited him there, which he accepted of, arriving at Rheims, December 1, 1590, and whilst he remained on visit there he was pleased to perform the office of a catechist in which he so much delighted.*

Mr. Wood † thus speaks of Father Darbyshire—
"In the beginning of Queen Elizabeth he was deprived of his spiritualities, whereupon Thomas Cole, who had been Dean of Salisbury, as 'tis said, in the time of King Edward VI., and afterwards an exile in the time of Mary, succeeded him in his archdeaconry, who kept it till the time of his death, the beginning of 1571. After Darbyshire

---

* Dodd's *Church History*, vol. ii., p. 524. Edit. 1739. Mr. Dodd also says, quoting Wood's *Athen. Oxon*, p. 160, that Father Thomas had a brother, William Darbyshire, who was also a canon of St. Paul's, and died July 3, 1552.

† Wood's *Athen. Oxon*, vol. i., p. 83, Fasti. Edit. 1721.

was deprived, he went beyond the seas, and at length entered himself into the Society of Jesus, and became a noted person amongst the Roman Catholics. He had a great skill in the Scriptures, and was profound in divinity. He catechised also many years publicly at Paris in the Latin tongue with great concourse and approbation of the most learned of that city. Whether he wrote anything, I find not as yet, only that he died at a good old age at Pont-a-Mousson, 1604 (2 James I.). Whilst he was chancellor of the diocese of London, he had much to do in examining heretics, as they were then called, that were brought before Bishop Bonner about matters of faith." So far Mr. Wood.

To return to the thread of our narrative. Father Darbyshire, before his noviceship was ended, being asked, according to custom, if he was ready to undertake the duty of teaching in any class, even the lowest, and for as long as obedience should enjoin him to do so, and also to perform any duty, however low, that might be assigned him, he gave the following answer in writing—*Paratum cor meum Deus, paratum cor meum; neque dubito verum dixisse Christi vicarium in initiis hujus Societatis, quando ista protulit, Digitus Dei est hic*—"My heart is ready, O my God, my heart is ready; nor do I doubt but that the Vicar of Christ spoke the truth when, in the commencement of this Society, he uttered these words, 'The finger of God is here.'"

He was sent to Dillingen, where for some years

he spread the sweet odour of his virtues. Whilst at Dillingen he was, according to Sacchinus,* sent to Scotland in 1566 on some mission by the Holy Father, as companion (with Father Edmund Hay, then Rector of the Scotch College, Paris) to the Apostolic Nuncio, Vincentius Laurens, whom the Pope had consecrated Bishop, and appointed as his own successor in the see of Monte Regale. The object of this mission does not appear, though it was probably connected with some affairs of Mary Queen of Scots, who was married to Darnley the following year. From Dillingen he was ordered to France, having been appointed Master of Novices at Billon, in the exercise of which most responsible office he displayed specimens of every virtue, both in the art of discernment of spirits (in which he was specially distinguished), and being possessed of the most affable manners, he applied himself to every duty of conciliating and conserving, and the exercise of works of benevolence and charity. Father Darbyshire was solemnly professed in the Society of Jesus in the year 1572. For some years he lectured in Latin to the members of the Sodality of the Blessed Virgin.†

As no leave had been given, until 1580, for any members of the Society to enter England, such being

---

* *Hist. S.J.*, pars iii., l. ii., n. 6.

† This would probably have been at Paris. Amongst the State Papers, *Dom. Eliz.*, 1574, Vol. xcix., No. 55, is a list of recusants names, and (*inter alios*), "Father Darbishere, Jesuite, Paris."

the inscrutable providence of God, Father Darbyshire, eager for procuring the salvation of souls in any place or country whatever, was employed entirely in assisting his neighbour in France, labouring especially amongst the lower classes and the ignorant, and though of such rare talents and a Professed Father in the Society, leaving the pulpits and chairs of professors, he almost entirely confined himself to giving catechetical instructions. This extreme humility in so learned and so distinguished a Father, was so agreeable to God that in spite of his determination to confine himself to the poorest of the poor, the young and illiterate, men of the highest rank and distinguished for their learning, flocked in numbers to hear him. This was especially the case when at Pont-a-Mousson, where his lectures and instructions were interspersed with displays of such ornaments of learning and eloquence, that not only his poor hearers were delighted, but grave theologians also would eagerly make notes of them, lest they should be lost when once delivered, being, as they said, worthy of a larger theatre.

In Paris an event occurred worthy of notice as a proof of his zeal, and in commendation of his admirable tact in leading the souls of men to God.

A certain English doctor in theology, cast forth from his native land by the common shipwreck of schism, arrived safely at Paris. He was an old friend of Father Darbyshire, who frequently visited him, and resolved to attack him upon the point of making

P

his confession, and to persuade him to make a general one of his whole life. Therefore, taking a favourable opportunity, he began the subject; and, in order to draw his friend's attention in the right direction, he said, "I have nothing to do with other matters; this alone demands my only care. I had a dream last night which may equally strike you as wonderful, as it vehemently admonishes me of my duty. I seemed to be seated with a party at a lordly table, when, during the feast, musicians happened to enter the room. They asked if any one wished to hear some music? 'Certainly,' was the reply of all. Then one of them turning to me, said, 'Dost thou wish me to sing thee a song?' 'I give you leave,' I answered; 'sing on.' But the man, lifting up the veil of my conscience from my earliest years, placed at one view before my eyes all the sins I had ever committed up to that hour, which struck me with so great a horror that I resolved with all possible speed to free myself from the dreadful burthen. 'Come on, therefore,' said Father Thomas; 'take a quiet interval of two or three days in which to examine carefully your whole past life, that you may the more perfectly prepare yourself for so excellent a work.' 'This is not necessary,' he replied; 'for I always keep things so clearly digested in my mind that any such delay is superfluous.'" The doctor then and there, in an admirably arranged manner, made his general confession, giving us a lesson of the wonderful method by which God is pleased to assist His own elected ones; and it was for himself, as he little thought at the time, a preparation for a much nearer departure from this world than he expected, for soon after he was seized with mortal sickness and died piously.

To the industry of Father Darbyshire, says Tanner, England owes the conversion of Mr. George Gilbert (the second subject of this volume, who had been led into France, and visited Paris) from the errors of Calvin to the one true Church of God; and who was afterwards the faithful companion of Father Parsons, and rendered him and Father Edmund Campion, and the other Priests, such immense assistance in the salvation of multitudes of souls in England.

We may also add that to the same zeal and industry the Society of Jesus owes their renowned member, and the Catholic Church in Ireland its zealous labourer and confessor of the Faith, Father Henry Fitzsimon, whose most deeply interesting life, and one of such historical importance in the annals of Irish Church history, is at the present time being brought to the light of day by the labours of the Reverend Father Edmund Hogan, of the Irish Province of the Society of Jesus, in consecutive numbers of the *Irish Ecclesiastical Record*. In the following extract from Father Henry Fitzsimon's work, *Justification of the Masse*, chap. iii., p. 115: "Of holy water, and effects thereof"—in giving an instance of its miraculous effects upon himself, he alludes to his journey to Paris, where the supernatural event happened, and his conversion by Father Darbyshire—

"Yet truly Sathan and al his adherents have cause to detest holy water, whether antient Christians approved it or noe; considering that St. Eligius delivered fiftie possessed by devils by only sprinkling them therwith, and St. Gregory and St. Hubert purged monasteries and howses formerly subiect to their molestation in the same maner. Therwith also did our St. Malachie helpe and heale a woman in frensie and divers others diseased. Nether are more miraculous histories recorded of any other memorial of Christ's benifits toward vs. For the vse of *holie water* is to make vs myndful of our regeneration by the water of baptisme; as *holy bread* of our feeding on the B. Bodie of Christ Jesus; as the *Agnus Dei* of our deliverie by Christ's oblation for synns, and as the framing of the sign of the *Crosse*, of our triumph over death and hel, by Christ's holy Passion. They are therfor grateful memorials, because they are a kinde of real protestation of our myndful gratuitie; whereby also God maketh them soe miraculous, to warrant such our devotion, and to testifie His gratious acceptation.

"It is honorable to reveale the works of God, nor lesse in my owne cause then of others. I wil briefly relate it as a merciful worke of God with al humble and grateful fidelitie. In the year 1587, being twentieth of my age, and tenth of my education in heresie, I came to Paris; so far overweening of my profession, that I surmised to be able to convert to Protestancie any encountre whosoever. Nether did I fynde many of the ordinarie Catholikes, whom I did not often grauel. At length, by my happines, I was overcome by Father Thomas Darbishire, ane owld English Jesuit, long tyme experienced in the reduction of many thowsands to the Catholike religion.

"Only toward holy water I remained squeamish, I know not how; rather by ignorance than obstinate, or malitiouse doubtfulnes. At the same tyme a vehement tormenting payne seased my third finger of the left hand, with that smarting griefe that I thought often to chopp it of. No fomentation could qualifie it. A holy day requiring my going to Masse, I would not in the first fervour of my devotion omitte it, not knowing then but that I was bound thereto notwithstanding al paine. Repairing therfore to St. Severius' Church, my payne redubled in such scorching excesse that I teared and groned, as in the greatest agonie; and being neere the holy water font, I plunged in my whole hand, not then for devotion, but for refrigeration. To Thee, O Lord my God, be al prayse for ever and ever, who at that very instant vnsensiblie, intierly, abundantlye didst heale me without al sensible signe of my former payne, and with exclusion of al palenes and vncheerfulness thereby procured, in the presence of M. Henry Segrave, M. John Lea, M. Dominiche Roch, and many others, giving me occasion to be confounded for my incredulitie, and eternally thankful for my deliverance. To Thee, therfore, again and again, be al glorie for ever and ever. Amen!"

To his other labours Father Darbyshire was no less assiduous in the duties of the confessional; in which he not only applied himself to the conversion of great sinners with much zeal and industry, but God also was pleased to add to his efforts wonderful efficacy, and to enable him by prodigies also to assist his penitents.

During his residence in Paris he wrote the following beautiful letter to another member of the Society at Avignon. A copy in Latin is in the State Papers Office;* the original letter is preserved in the British Museum, Harlein MSS., Vol. cclxxxviii., fol. 154. In another hand at the top of the letter is written, "The vain hope the Papists had of the King's apostacy." The original letter is endorsed, "Father Darbyshire—intercepted letter." To have intercepted a letter written in France to another party in the same country shows the extraordinary activity of the Government spies in those times.

The copy in the Public Record Office is endorsed, "Coppye of a letter of Darbishier to another English Jesuite at Avignon, whereof I have sent the original to Mr. Secretary, 29th August, 1584."

"I have received your letter of the 6th of the nones of July, which afforded me the greatest joy, as from it I learn that you persevere in your vocation,

* *Dom. Eliz.*, Vol. clxxii., No. 17, 1584.

and (as I hope) make progress, which I trust you will always do. That you are mindful of me for my good is what I give thanks for, first to God, and next to yourself, for so I persuade myself it will be. On many accounts I confess that I am bound to you, nor shall you find me ungrateful in anything in which I may be able to serve you. This, beyond measure delights me, that the mere recollection and thought of our Institute so pleases you. Believe me, my Brother, that this is a singular grace of God which not many receive. Oh! if we but knew the gift of God." [The letter then gives some information about one Henry Bayley in Paris, and continues]—" Your parents are well, but your father always in prison on account of his faith and profession of the Catholic religion. Oh! happy you to have such a father, so constant in the Faith, and so ready to die for Christ and His holy Catholic Church. It would be pleasing to them to receive letters occasionally from you; but I leave it to your prudence to be sure not to write to them anything that would make your father's condition worse as regards his bodily sufferings. We have here now, and for some months past, Father Robert Parsons, of whom you will have often heard, the companion of Father Campion. There is another Father also, Father Weston, who has come hither not long ago from Spaine. In this province we are nine Englishmen at present; praise be to Christ.

"Concerning England, I will only say this much, that those men are full of fury and full of fear, their wicked consciences giving them no rest. I do not see what they have to fear from man. Would that they strove to make God their friend.

"The King of Scotland [afterwards James I.] goes on well, but when I consider that his mother is in England [Mary, Queen of Scots, in prison], and that he is deprived of her wisdom and experience, and is without external help and advice, I fear much that some evil may happen, both for him and for us, for she who now reigns in England, as long as she [Queen Mary] lives, does not think herself secure, and will leave no stone unturned to get rid of her.*

"Edward, who a short time ago came from England into France, who was friendly to your father, is in prison for the Catholic business which is now being treated of.

"Farewell, and commend us to Christ in your prayers. Salute in my name, very affectionately, your Reverend Father Rector, of whom I have retained the most pleasant recollections.

"Yours always in our Lord,

"THOMAS DARBYSHIRE, Soc. Jes.

"Paris, 13th August, 1584."

* On the 8th of February, 1587, Mary Queen of Scotland and Dowager of France was beheaded at Fotheringhey Castle, Northamptonshire, by Elizabeth, after an imprisonment of eighteen years. As her constancy in the Catholic religion was the chief cause of her death, whatever might otherwise be pretended, so she is usually reckoned amongst those who suffered for religion (Challoner's *Missionary Priests*, vol. i., p. 191. Edit. 1741).

The following is a specimen of the spy system employed by the bitter anti-Catholic Government of the time, and shows to what a depth of degradation even a Sir Francis Walsingham could stoop to to curry favour in high quarters, and to entrap such a man as Father Darbyshire. We insert this letter without the slightest fear of damaging the character of that holy man, whose long and deep experience in the ways of the world, and in the trials of those times, and whose great prudence were proverbial, to say nothing of his well-known piety and sanctity of life. Let the candid reader contrast the Father's character with the barefaced statement of the spy, and of his honourable employer, and he will find but little difficulty in treating the whole (and this applies to the case of most of these spies) as a tissue of misstatements, or exaggerations, if not altogether a concoction of falsehoods, invented only to deceive and please the employer and turn the tables upon Walsingham himself, as tacitly, at least, suggesting the getting rid of Mary Queen of Scots, "Whose life is a steppe vnto her Majestie's death," and advising his Sovereign "for her own safetie and her subjects to add to God's good providence her just policie," &c.

Harlein MSS., 260, p. 178, *Plut.*, lxvi. E. British Museum. Sir Francis Walsingham to the Right Hon. Lord Burleigh.

"March 15th, 1572.

"To the Rt. Hon. and my very good Lord of Bourleigh.

"Your lordship, by Sir Thomas' letters unto her Matie., shal be fully informed what hath passed in conference, as wel with the Kinge as his deputies, touching the league to which I refer yow. Of late I caused one, under the colour of a Catholique, to repaire to one Darbyshire, an English Jesuite in Paris, for that I understand there is a concurrence of intelligence betweene him and those of Loraine, as also with those of the Scottish Queene's faction. The partie I sent did seeme [pretend] very much to bewaile the evill successe that the late practices took in Englande, and that nowe he did feare theire cause would growe desperate, especiallie for that Mathers' enterprize was alsoe discouvered. To this the Jesuite answered, that the evil handling of matters was the cause of that they tooke noe better effecte. Notwithstandinge, saith he, bee of good comforte, and assure yourselfe there are more Mathers in England then one, who will not omitt, when time shall conveniently serve, to adventure their lives in seeking to acquit us of that lewde woman [meaning Her Matie.], for, saith he, if she were gone, then would the hedge lye open, whereby the good Queen that now is prisoner, in whome resteth the present right of this crowne, should then safely enjoy the same. For besides that all the Catholykes which in the realme of England are at her devocon, there are, sayth he, diverse heretiques, God bee thanked, that are well affected towards her; which, sayth hee, is noe small miracle that God hath soe blinded theire eyes, as that they should bee inclined vnto her, that in the end shall yeelde unto them theire just desertes, unless they return to the Catholique faith. The other replied, that for his parte he coulde never hope to see her at libertie, nor longe to see her keepe her heade uppon her shouldiers, and therefore could receave no greate comforte that way. Well, sayth the Jesuite, I tell you trewlie that I dare assure yow shee shall have noe harme, for shee lacketh noe friendes in the English Courte, and as for her libertie (saithe hee), it standeth all good Catholiques in hande soe much to see it, eyther by hook or by crooke, as doubte not man; but there are some good men that will venture a joynt to bringe it to passe. For yf shee were once possessed of the crowne of England, it wil bee the onlie way and meane to reforme all Christendome in reducinge them to the Catholique faith, and therefore you must thinke that there are more heades occupyed in this matter then English heades, and that there are more waies to the wood than one, and therfore be of good courage, and ere over one yeare bee att an end, yow shall know more. Besides the villanous and undutyfull language of Her Matie., he used very lewd and bitter speeches agaynst the Earl of Leicester and your lordp. And this was the summe of theire talke, which I confirringe and weighinge with the former intended practices, made me thinke it worth the advertisement, that Her Matie. may see how much theye build uppon the possibilitie of that dangerous woman, whose life is a stepp vnto Her Mtie.'s death, for that they repute her for an undoubtfull successor, or raither, which is a more danger, for a right inheritour. And though I know her mischievous intencons are limitted, that they reach no further to Her Mtie.'s harm or prejudice then shall seeme good to God's providence, yett is Her Mtie. bound, for her own safetie and her subjects, to add [to] the same His good providence, her just policie, soe farr forth as may stand with justice. And soe leavinge further to trouble your honour att this present, I most humblie take my leave.

"Att Sloys, the second of Marche, 1572,

"Yr. honour's to commande,

"FFRANCIS WALSINGHAM."

The following is an extract from a letter of one Henry Alis, another Government spy.[*] He says (*inter alia*)—"That, being bound for Paris, he was commended from John Woodward unto Pater Thomas Darbysher, one of the Fathers of the Jesuetts of Paris; who acquainted me with one James Hill, servant unto the Duke of Guise, and hath a brother that doth serve my Lord of Arundell. Also, he acquainted me

[*] *Domestic, Eliz.*, State Papers, P. R. O., 1588, Vol. ccix., No. 57.

with one Robert Tempest, that is Treasurer and Procurator of the Colledge of Reims; and, after divers communications passed betwixte us, and he knowinge by the reports of my Lord of Northumberlande's younge sonnes and their tutor that are in Paris, and one Thomas Hole that was tutor to my Lord of Northumberlande that nowe is, gave me creditt the better. And when I was in the Marshalsea, of your honor's commandment, I was acquainted with diverse Prestes that were banished owte of the Marshalsea, and are now in Paris. One Smith and one Griffen, and diverse other Prestes, which made me creditt the better; and, after many greate schoolings, with the fall of Gyfford, being alledged that he was a spy; and divers other admonitions for my loyaltie towardes theire Church," &c. [This spy, having thus got admittance to the Catholics, proceeds to give various information he had gathered. As regards Father Darbyshire it is very trifling, thus]— "Father Darbyshire began in this manner with me, and began to bewaile the state of our nobilitee, and wished to God they bore so noble a mind in England as the Duke of Guise doth, who had the Kinge up in a mewse, and perforce made him swear and agree to what they wolde, or else he sholde be put where two or three Kinges had been before—in a Religious howse, and so ended their daies."

Having given the two foregoing specimens of the plans of the Government spies connected with the subject of our history, the reader must pardon a short digression here upon this interesting subject, by introducing the account of a notorious spy, a *pious evangelical* character, who actually made his way into the English College at Rome, and there pretended to become a convert to the Catholic faith. These men penetrated, under all imaginable shapes, into prisons, private and Religious houses, and Colleges at home and abroad, so that a Catholic of whatever degree was never secure. In the P. R. O., State Papers, *Dom. Elizabeth*, Vol. cxlix., No. 184, is the following (endorsed "Secret advices—Samuel Postinget ")—

"Whereas, your honor desireth to knowe all such manor of dealinges as the Papists do use towards Protestantes for to make them denye their Lord and Maker, and so to revolte from their fayth. . . . I sett forth unto you ther behaviour towardes me and my felowe in our aboad there amongst them.

"First, therfore, when wee came to Rome we wente unto the English Seminarye ther, and wherās to others the preveledge of the house go but viij dayes, yet beinge we were scholars, yonge men in necessitie, and not instructed in ther religion, they granted unto us vj weekes at the leaste, in which tyme they did nothing but persuade us for to be reconciled to ther Churche, and to become (as they call them) Catholiques. We had a booke or two which they tooke from us, and instead of them gave us such bookes as best pleased ther myndes, in the which we learned Seaven Sacraments; workes without fayth to be sufficient to salvation; the Pope to be the Head of the Churche, and that whatsoever he did binde and loose in earth the same was bound and loosed in Heaven; that whosoever dyed not in the state of ther Churche dyed not in the state of grace, and so could not be saved. Of Purgatory, also, there was somewhat to be seene, and how in the Sacraments we did eate and drinke the Body and Blood of Christ wholly and substantiallye, with an infinite companye more of such devilishe doctrines, amongst Christians never to be named. Thus, when they had *nortered* [nurtured] us at ther pleasure a tyme, they called a Congregation, in the which the Pope gave us leave to be admitted into the bosome of ther Church. All this done, yet they could not admit us thereunto till such tyme as being ledd by feare, or compelled by force, they had made us to abjure ourselves, and utterly, to forsake God and His trewth. And, instead of this, to swear that forever we would follow ther religion, viz., Antichrist, &c.

"Now, when they had wrought us to ther purpose, as they thoughte, then we were amongst them confirmed, after that confessed and pardoned our sins by a man who hath no lesse need to have his sins washed away in the blood of Christ then we had, and thus they doe with all such that come hither. . . .

"Further more, whereas your honor commanded me to sett downe the names of all such as I did know beyond the seas, enemies to ther country and fled for religion. Although I cannot remember all ther names, yet the names of those I do know I will rehearse as trulye as I can."

The spy then proceeds to give a very long list of Priests and others in the English College, &c., Rome. He then proceeds thus—

"Ther be 20 more in the Sem. at Rome, at the leaste, whose names I know not. Paris doth abound with Papists, and I am persuaded that his honor the L. Ambass. hath and doth seeke all possible meanes to roote them owte yf it could be; and refuseth neyther coste nor labour to winne them (if they woulde hear him) unto the Shepherd of their sowles Ct. J., and obedience towards ther Prince and countrye."

This spy then proceeds, by command of his honour, the Secretary, to point out the means for obtaining news from Rome. He names an Italian Catholic, who loveth England, and married an Englishwoman, one John Brygosa. Also one William, an Englishman, who had married an Italian. Also a young man, Edward Boss, once a scrivener in London, who made his way to Rome, and got into the Inquisition, &c. &c. He also told the Lord Ambass. "of 3 other verye fytt men to be spyes," with whom his honor must find some one to speak about it. He goes on—

"This much I certified my L. Ambass. more, that many he might thither sende, but some or none of them should ever come away, for yf he be known to have been in France, though he never came in England (or at the least not of two or three years), and goeth not from D. [Douay], often letters are at Rome afore him for his apprehendinge when he cometh thither.

"I further certifye his honor that yf these before rehearsed were not sufficient instruments to bring to pass his honor's purpose, then yf he did please to fynd out the man, I wolde sett downe the course he should take, which yf he wolde observe, he sholde live in Rome a spye so longe as him listed: and moreover that yf no meanes colde be founde to convey letters I wolde shew unto his honor howe a man should goe thither, and retorne agayne at his pleasure, without all suspycion. His honor inquired not of me the meanes how this might be wroughte, onlye he willed me to advertize yr honor thereof, when I come to London. To show myselfe obed. therefore unto his honor's comandment I assure your honor that yf all occasyons of hearing newes from Rome, were taken away (as I think they be well nere), yet your honor may betraye the same by pilgrimage.

"Last of all I gave his honor to note of one Pownde, a Pryste bound for Inglande. He came from Rome in the beginning of Lent, and I did think he woulde have gone by Paris, which yf he did I told his honor that in my opynion noe greater benefit colde be wroughte to our countrye then to worke his apprehendinge. He ys a very weake man, and such an one as I thinke according to the proverbe, had rather 'turne than burne,' which yf he coulde be broughte unto, yt wolde greatlie worke the confusion of the Papystes, for that ys one of the things that they doe chiefly boaste of, namelye, that as yet none of their Priestes have fallen or recanted.

He then proceeds to point out, "in obedience to your honor's comand, the things which doe most hurt the estate of our countrye," and his opinion as to the remedye.]

"Fyrste, therfore, that matters in Council privately handled must be privately kept, and not imparted but unto those which love their countrye, and the good estate thereof, for I protest unto your honor that ther is nothinge done in your Privie Council which is not known in Rome within 8 wekes at the moste, and this I think one inconvenience, but as touchinge the remedye thereof, I leave that to your honor.

"Another inconvenience is the lyfe of Parson, a Jesuit, who hurteth our countrye more than I am able to declare, onlye I note the same unto your honor as one great hurte unto our countrye, and to be forseen by your honor's wisdom.

"Another inconvenience ys as I thinke the continuance of the English Seminarye at Rhemes, a thing very easy to be reformed, and no small benefite unto our comon wealth, for yf it were made frustrate, the

Seminarye at Rome were to no effecte. I could laye down some reason for that which I doe saye, but your honor's wysdom is able to comprehend the sume of my meaninge.

"Another inconvenience is that Papistes are suffered to live in the Inns of Court (I dare not say in the Queen's M^tie's Court) lest I shoulde offend, but this I dare boldlye saye that amongst lawyers more Papystes ther are than in all Inglande beside, for yee have not nowe allmoste in Englande one Papist Priest which hath not been a lawyer, or els broughte upp amongst them.

"Another discomoditie ensueth by givinge unto young gent^n leave to travell beyond the seas under the pretence of learning language, were yt not for discharge of my conscience, and for shewing my betrothed dutye unto your honor, I had rather with sylence to overpasse these thinges, then otherwyse to deal with them, fearing that if it were known I should have small rewarde for my labours.

"Another inconvenience is yt your searchers are not trustye; they covet all to be gent^n and yf at the first entering to their office they be not worth a groate, within a yeare or two they become so ryche that they will be purchasers. This is not by just dealinge," &c.

To return to Father Darbyshire. Father John Gerard in his narrative* mentions that he became

---

* See Father Morris' valuable work, *Condition of Catholics*, &c., pp. xii., xiii.

acquainted with Father Darbyshire during the residence of the former at Clermont College, Paris, about 1582-3. "After my residence at Rheims I went to Clermont College, Paris, to see more closely the manner of the Society's life, and to be more solidly grounded in humanities and philosophy. I had not been there one year when I fell dangerously ill. After my recovery I accompanied Thomas Darbyshire to Rouen, in order to see Father Parsons, who had arrived thither from England, and was staying *incognito* in that city to superintend the publication of his *Christian Directory*, a most useful and happy work, which in my opinion has converted to God more souls than it contains pages."

We have before mentioned that Father Darbyshire was obliged to leave Paris on account of ill health. He again visited Rome, and then went to Pont-a-Mousson, in Lorraine. There he remained until his death. He received the following most interesting letter at Pont-a-Mousson from Father Henry Tichbourne. This letter was probably intercepted; at all events by some means it has found its way to the State Paper Office.*

---

* *Dom. Eliz.*, 1598, State Papers, Vol. cclxii., No. 28. Father Henry Tichborne, of Salisbury, entered the Society of Jesus October 11, 1587. He rendered essential service to the rising English Seminary at Seville, founded by Father Parsons in 1588, as Minister, Confessor, and Professor of Moral Theology. Father Henry More (*Hist. Prov. Angl.*, p. 290), fixes his death in the year 1606, and adds that he died "with a great opinion of his sanctity and learning."

"The reasons that moveth us in these partes to have hopes more then ordenare of ye convercōn of our contrye are verie pregnant. Firste, ye hie degree of credit our princepal pilleirs and agentes have bothe in R[ome] and S[pain]. In R——, Fr. P[ersons] with the Pope himselfe is so accepted that he will not suffre him to use anie other complimente of *Kinghes* or other wayes in his presence then are usual for Cardinalles: his nevew hath assigned him his day of audience, and sendeth his coche for him dailie: he hath composed those desperate controversyes between the Fathers and Scolerres and let out ye corrupt bloode w^h that dexteritie as hath gott him ye fame of an expert phisitian; and hath triumphed so over ye crue of malcontentes that whereas before his coming to R———, ye young youghters [youngsters] were so averted from the S[paniards] that they could not abide ther sight, and wold not move ther hattes to the Ambassd: he brought them to degest the one, and respect the other. And to confirm me ye rather in this opinion, I find that with great difficultie and the clamorous reluctation of our hole [whole] Ordre he hath avoided the reade cappe, Ffr. C[reswell] in S[pain], and Ffr. H[olt] in Flanders have with ye Princes they deal with no less credit then he here. The seconde supporte of this our hopes yr ye continuallie confiuence of the rares and bestes wittes of our nation to the Seminaires, and ther constance in following their missions, and procuring to be qualified for ther retorne; which ys in ye sight of man marvellous to se that ye rigoure of ye lawes conceavid and contrived in those cases and ye vigilant ayes [eyes] and sever execution ther of thes ten or xii yeares practised hath bene ye foundacion of all this our credit abrod and an invitement to men to adventure for God's sake and ye saving of soules, ther skinne and bones. It ys then observid yt where before these lawes published, we had but tow [two] Seminaries, and those but indeferantlie fornished of persons or provision, sens that tyme for tow we have 8 : one here the nombre 70: one in Doyai the nombre 120: one in St. Omers the nombre 80. One in Vaillolit the nombre 63 : one in Civille the nombre 65; in St. Luca and Lisbonnd tow residences furnished proportionable and for our missions, wher before those onlie there retorned not 7 or 8 yearelie at ye most, now ye nombre of them yt retorne yearlie ys conted to be some 40 or 50. The nombre of adventurers and labourers in England is lifted to five hundred, besides them of our Societie which are some 150 in England and abrode, besides Capuchins and other Relegeux ye nombre of one 100. Thes evident testimones of missions and remissions and of ye particular intellegences of all preparations and pretentions of our Conseil at home sent continuallie to Fr. P. by expresse messingers yt all such that seke to contradict or oppose against him are ether discardid or discredited, and all they can say or projeecte to ye contrarie, held for inventions and intertainments. The onlie thing yt ys feared will be the interruption of this our settled hopes or diminution of credet ys a reporte which hath bene here verie herte [hurtful] of libertie of conscience at home, which is supposed to proceed from some deiper brayne then our ordenarie wittes are wonte to yealde; and because I knowe it will be to you gratefull and withall a caveat to take hede of such compaignons yt gape after yt libertie, I will set you downe ye discourse *pro* and *con*, and raisons upone bothe partes in ther memoriales for ye procuring of aprobation and good liking of ther designe. And first it was on both partes for a maxime concluded that parcial or propocinable execution of the lawes served for nothing els but to make suche as riped benefit therby reputed for spies, and men of so large a conscience, and in fine so hard to distinguish therin by the rule of more moderate execution that happilie those that lest deserved it were most hardlie dealte with. Yt rested then yt of late some by some publique altering and repealing of lawes or some solemne securitie under the Prince's worde yt ys objected on the one parte and much feared of ours yt this ys the onlie meanes to discover the defeate and nakednes of our cause and to show that yt which we are faine to doute wth suche gloriose colours ys but a mere chemire [chimera] and bare shadowe, yt ther is no suche nombers of men affected to our parte as we wolde enforce yt a more milde and moderate course were more fetting for all partes that yt ys observed in all histores yt religion was never planted or restored by armes; that suffering and submission must nedes in tyme worke commiseration. That liberty granted will be a badge and as yt were a leverie cote to distinguish betweene staide and plaine meaning Catholiques, yt are desirous to geve Cæsar yt which ys Cæsar's, and God yt which ys God's, yt ye way to take away on all partes geloses, suspitions, and a laborinth of perplexites ys for the one part to geve what testimonie or pledge may humanlie be devised by ther innocence and sincere submission, ye other of ther humanitie, nobilitie, and obedience, yt for obtaining this liberte they offer no other conditions than Card! Allain dothe in his apologe *Tertullian and Justinius Martyr*. Replie was made by ours that this meanes was so dangerous yt what rigour of lawes cold not compasse in so manie yeares, ys liberte and lenitie will effectuate in 20 dayes. To wit the disfernishing of ye Seminaries, the disanimating of men to come, and others to retorne; ye expultion of the Societie a confusion as in Germanie; extinction of zeal and fervor a disanimation of Princes from the hott pursuit of ye enterprise of our reduction, will leave us hopeles and healples and will fall out with us as with the shepe yt maid peace with the wolves on condition they should remove the dogges. So that the circumstances and conditions necessarielie imply the removal of the Companie (wch by ther rule may admitte no like conditions) and are our dogges. We shall be left as a praye to ye wolves yt will besides drive our greatest patron to stoupe to a peace wch will be the utter ruine of our edifice, this manie yeares in building. It was further opposed that color of matter of State was pretended, but ye marke was utterlie to extirpat and cut off by the rootes all memorie of ye Catholik religion, that the danger of suche alterations in a setled course the discredit might light upon ye devisers and makers of suche lawes yf suche mutations should now folow dothe demonstrate that this discourse of liberte ys but an invention of busie heades, and nether for to be allowed nor accepted yf it might be procured, nor in ytself possible to be procured, for the former raising hiatus was made that wisemen consider the end of the lawes and are not alwayes tied to the same meanes, but like skilfull phisitians use cupping or cutting but when otherwise the humours cannot be removed by potions and pourgalions; so that when Lycurgus' lawes may accomplish ther endes, they put into the scabbord the sworde of Draco's lawes till the rigours of tymes otherwise require. Seeing then yt by a benefit bestowed by repealing rigorous lawes, by using benignant and benificõus, by geven a limited and conditionall liberte the end of the law may take place wch ys to protect the State from perils and perturbances, to purge it of practitioners and intestine and domestical enemies, to flanke it and fortifie yt from all foraine invasions, yt ys thought yt no private love of estimation or affection to ther owne plottes which might grievouslie hinder so clement a mutation. To this replie was maid in a word yt ye world did"

[MS. damaged by age for three or four words] "the conservation of State as hatred of religion. It being further demanded with what credit the partie persecuting could be induced to suche alteration, or what securitie mght be required or geven of the partie benefitted, answere was made yt ye intercession of Princes in religion Catholik yet frendes to the State might make the alteration most honorable. Ther wordes likewise geven for the security might be considered sufficient, other particularities concurrent. None to be admitted or permitted to that benefit, but such as be men knowne to be faithful to the State should be approved, none but such as shall take othe to be free from matters of State and bound to reveale what they knowe to be prejudicial therto; and here by the way I must advise you that Sir Thomas Tresham as a frend to the State ys holden among us for an Atheist, and all others of his humour eyther so or worse. Thus you have what was argued on both partes : but the Libertins with ther raisons were with just disdaine rejected, so that I thinke hereafter they deare no more open ther mouthes.

"R[ome] this 2 of Febr., 1598.

"Yours ever assured,

"HENRY TWETCHBOURNE,

"of ye Societie of Jesus.

"Al molto R.do Padre il Pad.,Thomaso Derbeshire de la Comp.a de Giesu, a Mosseponti."

Father Darbyshire suffered grievously from some severe and obstinate disease in the shin bone which caused him acute pain and defied all the efforts of the medical men of the time, so much so that, despairing of any remedy, they decided that it was necessary to amputate the diseased limb, but Father Thomas imploring the aid of the Prince of the Apostles, on whose feast the terrible decision was come to, was suddenly cured by his powerful intercession.

It pleased God also to confer upon him the supernatural gift of the foreknowledge of events, of which the following is a remarkable instance. When the Fathers of the Society were assembled at the General Congregation in Rome for the election of a successor to Very Reverend Father General Mercurian, then just dead, Father Darbyshire who was then living at Paris, asked Father James Tiry, who was a Father of great authority and distinction in the Society, whether he knew a certain Father of the name of Claudius in Rome? To whom Father Tiry replied, "Certainly, I know him; but why do you ask?" Father Darbyshire then with childlike simplicity, relating what had occurred, said, "I arose at night to pray to God for the happy election of our new Father General, when the most clement Mother of God was pleased to condescend to appear to me, and conducted me in spirit to the conclave of the Fathers; then amongst the rest she led by the hand a certain young Father of the name of Claudius, and indicated to the Congregation that he was to be the object of their choice." The event proved the truth of his prediction, for shortly afterwards, Father Claudius Aquaviva was elected General, to the great advantage of the Society, and the no slight proof of the pious life and sanctity of Father Darbyshire.

None of Father Darbyshire's chroniclers even lead to the supposition that he ever returned to labour in the English mission. The following notices of a Priest of that name are found amongst the State Papers. They may refer to some other of the same name, or it is not an impossibility that this most zealous lover of souls may have again for a short time revisited his beloved and afflicted land. The exact date seems to be uncertain. The editor of the volume of State Paper *Calendars* puts "1584?". The extracts are given, and the reader left to form his own conclusion.

State Papers, *Dom. Eliz.*, Vol. clxviii., No. 33.

Endorsed—"An abstract of the notes delivered by the Lord Hunsdon concerning Seminarists and Recusants. Feb., 1583.

"The names of certaine persons noted in sondrie Counties to be Receavors and Entertayners of Jesuites and Seminaries [*inter alios*]—

"Mr. E. Ludlow of Cames, prisoner in Winchester. His wife keepeth in his house Gardiner, receiveth Darbyshire, *alias* Escham. S. Hampton.

"Mr. Wells of Otterbourne often harboureth in his house, Darbyshire, *alias* Hampshire, *alias* Escham. S. Hampton.

"City of London. At the house of Mr. Shelley of Mapledurham, County Southampton, are comonly to be found (amongst others) Derbyshire."

Father Darbyshire died at Pont-a-Mousson, on the 6th day of April, 1604, at the age of eighty-six.

www.ingramcontent.com/pod-product-compliance
Lightning Source LLC
Chambersburg PA
CBHW032135230426
43672CB00011B/2341